DATE DUE	
Krauthen due Nov 29/01		
APR 0 9 2003		
OCT - 3 1996	NOV - 5 1996	
OCT 17 1996	NOV 27 1996	
Oct 22	JAN 0 6 1999	
NOV 0 4 1996	MAR 1 4 2000	
DEC 0 2 1996	MAR 3 0 2000	
DEC 2 0 1996	OCT 1 9 2000	

OXFORD PSYCHIATRY SERIES

Searching for the Causes
of Schizophrenia

OXFORD PSYCHIATRY SERIES

Edited by
Joseph Coyle
Michael Gelder
Samuel Guze
Robin Murray

This picture represents a goddess bestowing a pearl of wisdom upon the world—an allegory of the cause of schizophrenia. It was given to the author by a psychiatrist from Beijing who was attached to the unit at Northwick Park.

Searching for the Causes of Schizophrenia

EVE C. JOHNSTONE

*Professor of Psychiatry and Head of Department of Psychiatry
The University of Edinburgh*

Oxford   New York   Tokyo
OXFORD UNIVERSITY PRESS
1994

Oxford University Press, Walton Street, Oxford OX2 6DP
Oxford   New York   Toronto
Delhi   Bombay   Calcutta   Madras   Karachi
Kuala Lumpur   Singapore   Hong Kong   Tokyo
Nairobi   Dar es Salaam   Cape Town
Melbourne   Auckland   Madrid
and associated companies in
Berlin   Ibadan

Oxford is a trade mark of Oxford University Press

Published in the United States
by Oxford University Press Inc., New York

A catalogue record for this book is available from the British Library

Library of Congress Cataloging in Publication Data
Johnstone, Eve C.
Searching for the causes of schizophrenia / Eve C. Johnstone.
(Oxford psychiatry series; 2) (Oxford medical publications)
Includes bibliographical references and indexes.
1. Schizophrenia–Pathophysiology. 2. Schizophrenia–Genetic
aspects. 3. Schizophrenia–Etiology. I. Title. II. Series.
III. Series: Oxford medical publications.
[DNLM: 1. Schizophrenia–physiopathology. 2. Schizophrenia–
etiology. WM 203 J73s 1994]
RC514. J585   1994   616.89'82071–dc20   93–42493

ISBN 0 19 262296 X

Typeset by The Electronic Book Factory Ltd, Fife, Scotland

Printed in Great Britain by
Biddles Ltd, Guildford & King's Lynn

Preface

This book serves two purposes. On the one hand, it is an account of the developments in biological research in schizophrenia over the past 20 years and an up-to-date assessment of the state of the art at present. On the other, it is a more personal description of my experiences while working in the Division of Psychiatry at the Clinical Research Centre, Northwick Park Hospital, UK.

During the time that I was there, extensive and far-reaching research into schizophrenia was conducted. I was the main clinical investigator in many of the studies. I hope that the description of my close acquaintance with the patients will offer the reader a more personal insight into the fascination and poignancy of the study of this enigmatic disorder.

Edinburgh   E.C.J.
April 1994

Acknowledgements

Much of the work with which the book is concerned was conducted when I worked at the Division of Psychiatry, the Clinical Research Centre, Northwick Park Hospital. I am deeply grateful to the Medical Research Council for giving me the chance to work in that stimulating and rewarding setting. None of the work would have been possible without the guidance, support, encouragement, and practical help of my friends and colleagues there. I would particularly like to acknowledge my debt of gratitude to Sir Christopher Booth and Dr K. Kirkham, Directors of the Clinical Research Centre, Dr T.J. Crow, Head of the Division of Psychiatry, and my many collaborators, especially, in alphabetical order, J.F.W.D., I.N.F., C.D.F., J.F.M., and D.G.C.O.

Contents

1

Introductory overview

Schizophrenia is a severe and often crippling mental disorder. It is relatively common. Typically, it first develops in early adult life and complete lasting recovery is unusual. It was first defined about a hundred years ago and since then it has been extensively studied and many investigations have been conducted to try to find possible causes for this enigmatic condition. These remain uncertain, but over the past 25 years technical advances have allowed investigations that have greatly increased our understanding. It has been my good fortune to have been involved in research in schizophrenia during this time and most of this volume is an account of the developments that I have seen take place. This first chapter, however, is concerned with the historical background against which concepts of schizophrenia developed, and summarizes the progress of research in this area until about 1970.

Historical aspects of the development of the concept of schizophrenia

Madness is mentioned in ancient texts such as the Hindu Ayur Veda and the Old and New Testament. In the writings dating from the second century AD of Aretaeus the Cappadocian it is discussed at length. However, although the descriptions of melancholia and its switch into hilarity are easy to recognize as what would now be called bipolar affective disorder, there is no clear account of an illness that could readily be diagnosed as schizophrenic. Although Willis (1683) and Kinnear (1727) left descriptions of symptomatology that could have been due to schizophrenic illness, the first unambiguous descriptions to which such a diagnosis could reasonably be applied were written in 1809 by Haslam and by Pinel. Throughout the nineteenth century many attempts were made to classify insanity. In 1856 Morel introduced the term démence précoce to describe an adolescent patient, once bright and active, who had slowly lapsed into a state of withdrawal.

He gradually lost his cheerfulness, became gloomy, taciturn and showed a tendency towards solitude—the young patient progressively forgot everything he had learned, his so brilliant intellectual faculties underwent in time a very distressing arrest. A kind of torpor akin to hebetude replaced the earlier activity and when I saw him I concluded that the fatal transition to the state of démence précoce was about to take place . . . A sudden paralysis of the faculties, a démence précoce indicates that this patient had reached the end of his intellectual life that he can control.

Many other psychiatrists wrote descriptive accounts of the clinical pictures presented by their psychotic patients but in 1896 Emil Kraepelin, Professor of Psychiatry in Heidelberg and Munich, went beyond straightforward clinical description and divided the broad class of functional psychoses into two categories, essentially on the basis of outcome. The first category which he called manic-depressive insanity pursued a fluctuating course with frequent relapses but with full recovery between episodes. The second, for which he used Morel's term dementia praecox, embraced catatonia as described by Kahlbaum (1874), hebephrenia which had been described by Hecker (1871) and his own dementia paranoides. Kraepelin, grouped these together as different manifestations of a progressive disease which either pursued a steady downhill course to a state of chronic impairment, or if improvement did occur resulted only in partial recovery. In grouping together the mental illnesses of early adult life associated with poor outcome Kraepelin considered that he was defining a clinical syndrome which represented an disease of the brain the nature of which would be revealed by appropriate investigations.

In 1911 Eugen Bleuler published his *Dementia praecox or the group of schizophrenias* and it is his term of schizophrenia which has received general acceptance. Although Bleuler considered that he was developing Kraepelin's concept in fact he changed it substantially. Bleuler was influenced by psychoanalytic schools of thought and saw schizophrenia in psychological terms as much as in the neuropathological ones envisaged by Kraepelin. His term schizophrenia, meaning split mind, was intended to describe what he called a loosening of the associations between the different functions of the mind so that thoughts became disconnected and the co-ordination between emotional cognitive and volitional processes became poor. He considered thought disorder, affective disturbance, autism, and ambivalance to be the fundamental symptoms of schizophrenia and that the more clear-cut phenomena of hallucinations, delusions, and catatonic features emphasized by Kraepelin were of lesser importance. This view led him to conclude that schizophrenia could be diagnosed when there was no evidence that hallucinations or delusions had ever occurred and he thus added simple schizophrenia to the hebephrenic, catatonic, and paranoid forms recognized by Kraepelin.

Varying concepts of the disorder

Bleuler's term 'schizophrenia' became generally accepted and replaced Kraepelin's 'dementia praecox' and his ideas became influential in some centres, especially in the United States. However, Kraepelin's concept of dementia praecox, albeit under another name, as a disorder of uncertain or deteriorating course, generally poor prognosis, and probably based upon some as yet unidentified brain disease, never lost its domination in many European centres. The incompatibility of these two concepts of schizophrenia was illustrated by the findings of the US—UK diagnostic project (Cooper *et al.* 1972) in which substantial discrepancies between American and British psychiatric practice in the differentiation of schizophrenia from affective illness were highlighted. At a single hospital in New York and in London 250 consecutive admissions of patients between the ages of 20 and 59 years were studied. Structured interviews were conducted and standardized diagnoses made in accordance with internationally agreed criteria. The 'project diagnoses' obtained in this way were compared with the diagnoses given independently to the same patients by the hospital staff. In the New York series, 61.5 per cent of the patients were given a hospital diagnosis of schizophrenia, whereas in the London series the proportion was 33.9 per cent. However, in terms of the project diagnoses the percentages were 29.2 per cent and 35.1 per cent respectively. By contrast, 31 per cent of the London sample received a hospital diagnosis of manic-depressive disorder (depressive psychoses or mania) but only 5.2 per cent of the New York sample were given such a diagnosis. The conclusion is clear, the concept of schizophrenia in New York at this time was wider than that employed in London and this had occurred at the expense of affective disorder.

The distinction between the two major functional psychoses is not so readily made as has sometimes been assumed. Thus, the notion that in the affective disorders, psychotic phenomena (i.e. delusions or hallucinations) can be seen as secondary to the disturbance of mood, whereas in schizophrenia this is not the case, is no more than a rough generalization. It has long been recognized (Kasanin 1933) that a substantial proportion of functionally psychotic patients do not fit neatly into either category, having features considered typical of both schizophrenia and manic-depressive psychoses.

These findings and others have encouraged the formulation of operational rules for defining schizophrenia. Such systems specify whether or not an individual patient will be placed within that particular definition of schizophrenia according to the presence or absence of a given set of features. In spite of Bleuler's views, in the last 20 years the diagnosis of schizophrenia has generally been considered only in the presence of psychotic features, i.e. delusions, misperceptions, and/or thought disorder.

Table 1–1 *Three features of schizophrenia*

1. The presence of specific types of delusions or hallucinations or thought disorder, e.g. Schneider's (1957*b*) first rank symptoms.

2. The absence of primary mood change.

3. Chronic deterioration of function.

Once these features are present three separate areas of dysfunction may be used in making the decision that a patient has schizophrenia (See Table 1.1). Symptoms of the the first rank (also known as nuclear symptoms) were defined by Kurt Schneider (1957*a*, *b*) (See Table 1.2). According to Schneider these symptoms (Table 1.2) by themselves could identify an illness as unequivocally schizophrenic (although the force of this assertion was somewhat diminished by the recognition that they can occur in some other conditions such as amphetamine psychosis and the psychoses of temporal lobe epilepsy). Although Schneider denied that these symptoms necessarily had a particular significance in relation to the nature of the disease process and indeed regarded them merely as a pragmatic basis for diagnosis, several (e.g. 1, 4, 5, 6, and 8 in Table 1.2) relate to the peculiarly schizophrenic experience in which the contents of consciousness can arise from or be directly influenced by agencies other than the self. The areas of dysfunction listed in Table 1.1 bear no clear-cut relationship to one another and a concept such that the more typically Schneiderian the features the

Table 1–2 *Schneider's (1957a) 'symptoms of the first rank'*

1. Hearing one's thoughts spoken aloud in one's head.

2. Hearing voices arguing.

3. Hearing voices that comment on what one is doing.

4. Experiences of bodily influence (that bodily functions are affected by an outside agency).

5. Experiences that one's thoughts are withdrawn or that thoughts are inserted into one's mind.

6. Thought diffusion or the experience that one's thoughts are broadcast to others.

7. Delusional perception (the attribution of special significance to a particular perception).

8. Feelings or volitions experienced as imposed on the patient by others.

more clearly schizophrenic the illness would fly in the face of the facts. The operational definitions use the areas of dysfunction listed in Table 1.1 sometimes together with other features relating to age, family history, etc. In some systems, e.g St. Louis (Feighner *et al.* 1972), chronic deterioration is an obligatory feature while in others it is not. The relative weight given to the typically schizophrenic (essentially Schneiderian first rank) features and the absence of primary mood change may in theory range from:

first rank features = schizophrenia in all circumstances

to

any consistent mood change = affective diagnosis irrespective of the nature of the delusions and hallucinations

In practice, the Present State Examination (PSE) (Wing *et al.* 1974) and CATEGO programme emphasize first rank features while DSM III and DSM IIIR (APA 1980, 1987) are prepared to exclude more cases from a diagnosis of schizophrenia on grounds of an affective element.

There is no doubt that the operation of such rules to define the diagnosis of schizophrenia may greatly enhance reliability particularly when they are performed in association with a standardized interview (Leff 1977). Reliability in itself of course, may, be of no great advantage particularly if it is achieved within a framework of strict rules. In response to the same direct questions a patient with auditory hallucinations may deny to a series of observers that he hears voices. One hundred per cent reliability of diagnosis could be achieved based in every case upon misinformation. It is important not to lose sight of limitations of reliability and to recollect that operational criteria for individual diagnostic categories will give a clarity of separation of cases which may be a distortion of the reality of the situation. With this in mind it has been suggested (Cancro 1983) that the following verse could usefully be printed on every copy of DSM III.

That false secondary power
By which we multiply distinctions, then
Deem that our puny boundaries are things
That we perceive and not that we have made.
        Wordsworth—*The prelude, Book II*

Quite distinct from the question of reliability of diagnosis is the question of validity—that is, whether the diagnosis is a predictor of some independent variable such as outcome or response to treatment. Reliability sets a limit on validity but reliability may be high while validity remains low. A poor outcome is the variable most widely considered as a validating criterion for the diagnosis of schizophrenia and, indeed, for Kraepelin (1919) already was the defining characteristic of disorder. Outcome may be considered in terms of symptomatology and in terms of social functioning. Kendell *et al.* (1979)

have compared the validity of six operational definitions of schizophrenia by assessing their respective abilities to predict incomplete recovery from the episode, persistent symptoms, and poor social outcome. They found that all six definitions were more successful at predicting a poor symptomatic than a poor social outcome. Three sets of criteria—Langfeldt's (1960), Carpenter *et al.*'s (1973), and RDC (Spitzer *et al.* 1975)—consistently predicted poor outcome better than the presence of Schneider's first rank symptoms (1957*b*) or the New Haven criteria (Astrachan *et al.* 1972). This finding suggests that Schneider's first rank symptoms alone do not define the concept of schizophrenia as it has developed historically.

Early investigations of a possible biological basis for schizophrenia

With regard to aetiology, Kraepelin's view was that 'the causes of dementia praecox are at the present time still mapped in impenetrable darkness' (Kraepelin 1919: Barclay translation, p. 224). He did, however, devote a chapter of his book *Dementia Praecox* to morbid anatomy and quoted the work of Alzheimer (1897). He wrote 'The morbid anatomy of dementia praecox does not show macroscopically any striking changes of the cranial contents . . . On the other hand it has been shown that in the cortex we have to do with severe and widespread disease of the nerve tissue. Alzheimer has described deep-spreading changes in the cortical cells especially in the deep layers: The nuclei are very much swollen, the nuclear membrane greatly wrinkled the body of the cell considerably shrunk with a tendency to degeneration. Nissl invariably saw widespread cellular disease'. Although he believed the causes of the condition were unknown, Kraepelin considered that hereditary factors and 'injury to the germ' could be relevant. He postulated that 'such activities as are peculiar to the higher psychic stages of development' might be ascribed to the small-celled layers of the cortex noted to be damaged by Alzheimer, and stated: 'We see, therefore, in all the domains of psychic life the ancestral activities offering a greater power of the resistance to the morbid process than the psychic faculties belonging to the highest degrees of development'.

Sir Thomas Clouston saw adolescent insanity as being part of Kraepelin's concept of dementia praecox. Clouston, included adolescent insanity within his general concept of developmental insanity, and in his Morison lecture of 1890, he described investigations of palatal structure in adolescent insanity and other conditions. Clouston considered that his findings were an indication that adolescent insanity represented a form of developmental defect of ectodermal tissue (his results are shown in Table 1.3).

Many early investigations on the biological basis of schizophrenia

Table 1–3 *Frequency of the three types of palate in various classes of persons examined (Clouston, 1890)*

The different classes	No. 1 (Typical palate, %)	No.2 (Neurotic palate, %)	No.3 (Deformed palate, %)	No. of persons examined
The general population	40.5	40.5	1.9	604
Criminals (the degenerate)	22	43	35	286
The insane (acquired insanity)	23	44	33	761
Epileptics	20	43	37	44
Adolescent insanity	12	33	55	171
Idiots and imbeciles (congenital insanity)	11	28	61	169

From Clouston, T.S. (1890). Clinical lectures on mental diseases (6th edn). L and A Churchill, London.

concentrated on neuropathology and indeed the notion that the neuropathological changes were determined by maldevelopment of the brain was widespread (Mackenzie 1912; Turner 1912; Rosanoff 1914; Southard 1915). The early histological work of Alzheimer (1897, 1913), Wernicke (1900), Klippel and Llermitte (1909), described such changes as 'lacunae' pyknotic neuronal atrophy, focal demyelination, and 'metachromatic bodies'. However, this work was carried out when histological techniques were in their infancy and when the need for controlling fixation and staining was not appreciated. Such reports were questioned by Dunlap in 1924 in a careful comparison of the brains of eight schizophrenics (aged less than 45 years at death) with five controls selected in each case for having a cause of death unlikely to have influenced the structure of the brain. Dunlap arranged for cell counts in the areas where abnormalities had been described to be conducted by three independent observers. They were in good agreement and found no differences between patients and controls. Although histopathological studies of schizophrenia were continued by some workers, notably Cecile and Otto Vogt (Vogt and Vogt 1948), Dunlap's study cast a shadow of scepticism over this area of work which persisted for many years and is evident in later reviews, e.g. David (1957).

Although much of the early investigation concerned the structure of the brain a number of other areas were pursued. In general, these were not based on clear theoretical constructs but involved the application to the problem of schizophrenia of new methods of investigation as they developed. Gjessing (1938) described alterations of nitrogen metabolism in schizophrenic patients where illness took the form of relapsing and remitting catatonic symptoms—described as 'periodic catatonia', Lewis (1923) described a hypoplasia of the circulatory system in schizophrenics. Although Shattock (1950), who described peripheral vasoconstriction in schizophrenic patients, expressed the view that 'some of the abnormalities of behaviour observed in refractory patients may be related to a relatively inadequate cerebral circulation', Kety and Schmidt (1948) reported cerebral blood flow as normal. Kretschmer (1936) had related different types of mental disorder to different body builds and in fact Rees (1950) confirmed this but did find a considerable overlap in the distribution of physical types between manic-depressive and schizophrenic groups of patients. Numerous investigations of the endocrine systems in schizophrenic patients were conducted and, in particular, evidence of gonadal dysfunction was sought but the testicular abnormalies reported by Mott in 1919 and Hemphill *et al.* (1944) were not confirmed by the later work of Blair *et al.* (1952). Friedhoff and van Winkel (1962) and Bourdillon *et al.* (1965) found a substance which they identified as 3, 4-dimethyl-oxyphenylethylamine (DMPE) in the urine of schizophrenics. In the light of this the idea developed that abnormal methylation of catecholamines might be of aetiological importance for schizophrenia. However, the work of Keuhl *et al.* (1966) and Hollister and Friedhoff (1966) showed no support for this possibility. The careful review article by Kety (1959), which points out the numerous sources of artefact in schizophrenic patients is of relevance in considering these investigations.

Parallel to, but largely independent of, the neuropathological literature described above is a series of neuroradiological investigations of the brain in schizophrenia. Pneumoencephalography had been introduced by Dandy in 1919, and in 1927 Jacobi and Winkler claimed that 18 of 19 schizophrenic patients showed 'unquestionable' internal hydrocephalus. A number of other early studies were reported which had similar conclusions (Table 1.4), although most were uncontrolled. Pneumoencephalography is a procedure which can have serious effects in certain situations, and in 1929 the American Roentgen Ray Society declared that it was unethical to use normal controls in pneumoencephalographic studies. The propriety of this declaration is difficult to dispute but it did place limitations on the methodology of subsequent investigations. Some studies (Huber 1957; Haug 1962; Asano 1967) did, however, show relationships between ventricular enlargement and features of the clinical state within the schizophrenic group (Table 1.4). Some of the pneumoencephalographic studies were large, and evidently very well conducted. In general, in spite of the negative investigation of Storey (1966) the finding of ventricular enlargement in schizophrenia, and within groups of schizophrenic patients, of an association between such enlargement and features of deterioration and defect was confirmed.

Table 1–4 *Findings of pneumoencephalographic studies in schizo-phrenia*

Findings	Source
Unquestionable internal hydrocephalus in 18 of 19 cases.	Jacobi and Winkler (1927)
Increased size of ventricles and cisternae in 35% of 60 cases.	Moore *et al.* (1933)
Ventricular enlargement in 50% normals and 12% controls (100 cases examined).	Lemke (1935)
88% of 134 cases said to be abnormal.	Borenstein *et al.* (1957)
Dilated ventricles in 69% of 195 cases. Association of dilated ventricles with defect state.	Huber (1957)
Lateral ventricles larger in schizophrenia than controls (101 cases). Enlargement associated with clinical deterioration.	Haug (1962)
Cerebral atrophy in 58% of schizophrenics and 28% manic-depressives (260 cases).	Nagy (1963)
No significant differences between schizophrenics and normals negatively investigated for neurological disease (18 cases).	Storey (1966)
Lateral and third ventricle enlargement in 94% of nuclear and 43% of peripheral schizophrenics (53 cases).	Asano (1967)
Lateral ventricular enlargement in 52% of 27 cases (left-sided only in 33% of cases).	Hunter *et al.* (1968)
Atrophy in 24 of 36 schizophrenics referred for neurological assessment.	Young and Crampton (1974)
Ventricular abnormalities in 58 of 101 chronic schizophrenics previously studied (see above).	Haug (1982)

Social and other influences on the direction of research

It is not difficult to make the case that by the 1960s the pneumoencephalo-graphic results were the strongest evidence that there was in support of the view that there was a biological basis for schizophrenia and yet this evidence received little attention—indeed, in general it was ignored. In the light of later developments it seems strange that this should have been so but the general climate of opinion in the 1950s and 1960s and other aspects of the study of schizophrenia current at that time make this understandable. One simple reason for the relative neglect of this work is that little of it was accessible to those who could only understand English, but the fact that much of it was written in German is relevant for reasons other than language difficulties. Some of the work referred to earlier was, of course, conducted in Germany at the time of National Socialism. The findings could provide support for the view that schizophrenia was an inherited defect and be used in support of the eugenic and other policies put into practice at that time. The repugnance felt for these practices and the distaste for the fact that doctors had been involved in such behaviour made many reluctant to pursue this area of work or consider that any aspect of its basis could have been other than flawed. It is perhaps in part for these reasons that in the post-war period there was an upsurge of interest in psychodynamic and social psychiatry. The prevailing climate of opinion was that schizophrenia was a reaction to pathological relationships or patterns of communication within the schizophrenic's family. In 1948, Frieda Fromm-Reichman had coined the phrase 'schizophrenogenic-mother' and in 1956 Bateson *et al.* put forward the 'double bind' hypothesis of abnormal social interaction giving rise to schizophrenia. Lidz *et al.* (1965) conducted a descriptive study of the family life of schizophrenic patients in which they suggested that abnormal family interactions gave rise to schizophrenia. This work was highly influential although the studies were flawed in their methodology and have not stood up to scientific scrutiny (Hirsch and Leff 1975). Other work, of a high scientific standard is that of Wing and Brown (1961, 1970), the results of which remain influential—although recent attempts at replication have not been successful (Curson *et al.* 1992)—and it also weakened interest in the biological basis of schizophrenia. The possibility that institutional care might interact with the deficits of schizophrenia and intensify the social withdrawal and lack of motivation of patients with this disorder had been considered for some time (Myerson 1939; Martin 1955) but in 1959 Barton in his book *Institutional neurosis* expressed the view that these abnormalities could occur in anyone living for prolonged periods in such environments. The careful studies of Wing and Brown (1961, 1970) suggested that the psychological and social impairments of schizophrenic patients were partly the results of the circumstances in the institutions in which the patients lived.

Neuroleptic drugs were introduced into psychiatric practice in 1952 by Delay and Deniker. Their efficacy in treating acute episodes of schizophrenia was clearly demonstrated, a particularly well-conducted study being that of the Collaborative Study Group of the National Institute of Mental Health (NIMH) in 1964. At the time of the introduction of these drugs there was great optimism about their use and it was against this background that ideas were developed (Jones 1987) to the effect that most patients could be discharged from mental hospitals and no particular provision in the community would be required (Tooth and Brooke 1961; Taylor 1962). The thinking was that if schizophrenia was, in the first place, the result of abnormal patterns of family interaction in the patient's home, and the long-term disabilities were largely due to institutional care, the appropriate use of neuroleptic drugs would provide sustained symptomatic control. Thus, there would be no need for ongoing management for schizophrenic patients, and there would seem to be little purpose in looking for a biological cause for schizophrenia and a possibility of a structural genetic or developmental basis would seem to be unlikely. By the end of the 1960s when I first came into contact with schizophrenic patients, this high tide of optimism was beginning to recede in the face of the realities of non-response to treatment, the appearance of impairments in patients who had never been in institutions, and the difficulties of organizing the ideas of causative life experiences or imperfect family interactions into any testable hypothesis.

2

Opportunities provided by the technical advances of the 1970s

A number of technical advances were made in the 1970s and early 1980s that allowed hypotheses concerned with possible biological aspects of schizophrenia to be developed and tested.

Pharmacological and related advances

Although initial optimism about the long-term value of neuroleptic drugs in schizophrenia was not entirely justified there is no doubt concerning the efficacy of these drugs in relieving the positive symptoms of acute episodes in most schizophrenic patients (NIMH 1964). Psychopharmacological research in all areas had been driven in part by practical considerations of therapeutic benefits but much of the interest of this area comes from the idea that if a drug provides symptomatic relief of a condition then, because it acts on biological mechanisms, these mechanisms are likely to be operative in that condition. Indeed, the very existence of effective psychoactive drugs provides some sort of guarantee that biochemical and other biological mechanisms are important and perhaps crucial in at least some psychiatric illnesses. As far as schizophrenia is concerned the common pharmacological actions of the wide range of drugs effective in treating acute positive symptoms has led to substantial theoretical advances and to greater understanding of the disease.

Phenothiazine was used in the 1930s as an anti-helminthic in animals and a derivative promethazine was found to have powerful antihistaminic properties. In 1950, the closely related compound chlorpromazine was synthesized in France by Charpentier (Swazey 1974) and was found to have very powerful sedative properties inducing 'artificial hibernation' with retention of consciousness, marked indifference to surroundings, and hypothermia. These properties were first used in relation to anaesthesia but in 1952 Delay *et al.* introduced the drug into psychiatric practice. Although Delay and Deniker believed that chlorpromazine was actively anti-schizophrenic and not simply a super-sedative this idea was not initially widely accepted. By the late 1950s, however, large-scale trials in the United States showed clearly that barbiturate sedatives were no more effective than placebo in relieving schizophrenic symptoms, whereas phenothiazines were of consistent efficacy.

This discovery of a new class of drugs which relieved the fundamental symptoms of schizophrenia represented an enormous advance. A great deal of research effort has been devoted to understanding how phenothiazines and related anti-schizophrenic drugs act upon the brain. Soon after neuroleptics were introduced into psychiatric practice it was suggested that the anti-psychotic effect of these drugs was related to their ability to induce extra-pyramidal effects (Flugel 1953; Deniker 1960). Some, for example, Cole and Clyde (1961) and Bishop *et al*, (1965), doubted this on the basis that the extra-pyramidal effects of different neuroleptic drugs were not correlated with their anti-psychotic efficacy but this uncertainty appeared to be well-countered by the observation (Miller and Hiley 1974; Snyder *et al*. 1974) that drugs, such as thioridazine, with a low incidence of Parkinsonian effects, have high anti-cholinergic activity. The work of Hornykiewicz (1973) established that dopamine was depleted in the brains of patients who had died with Parkinson's disease. This is presumably a secondary consequence of degeneration of ascending dopaminergic pathways. Thus, the symptoms of Parkinson's disease seemed likely to be due to a failure of dopaminergic transmission. Selective effects of neuroleptic drugs on central dopamine turnover were described (Carlsson and Lindqvist 1963) and were attributed to dopamine receptor blockade. Thus, the extra-pyramidal effects of neuroleptics could be interpreted as a result of functional impairment of dopaminergic transmission. The development of *in vitro* assay systems for dopamine receptors has allowed extensive study of the dopamine antagonist effects of neuroleptic drugs. By the early 1970s, a number of different lines of evidence led to the conclusion that anti-schizophrenic drugs acted by blocking dopamine receptors in the brain. It was clear that what was needed to test this aspect of 'the dopamine hypothesis' of schizophrenia was the ability to assess the potencies of a wide range of anti-psychotic drugs as antagonists at dopamine receptors in the mamalian brain. This was not easy to do as such receptors have no obvious counterpart in peripheral tissues and assessing drug actions in the intact brain is very difficult since drug potency may be affected by metabolism or inadequate penetration into the central nervous system. It was therefore a major step forward when a simple biochemical model became available. The discovery by Kebabian *et al*. (1972) that dopamine-rich areas of brain contained a dopamine-stimulated adenylate cyclase allowed testing of the 'dopamine hypothesis' *in vitro*. The ability of phenothiazines to block adenylate cyclase paralleled the anti-psychotic efficacy of these drugs and this was also true of thioxanthenes like flupenthixol (Clement-Cormier *et al*. 1974; Miller *et al*. 1974). It was quickly recognized, however, that one important group of drugs, the butyrophenones such as haloperidol, did not fit into this model. These very potent anti-schizophrenic drugs were only weakly active in blocking the dopamine-cyclase response (Iversen 1975). It later became evident that the dopamine receptors which are coupled to cyclic AMP formation in the brain represent a particular pharmacological class, the D_1 receptor. The function of these receptors is uncertain and they are not apparently of crucial importance in the mechanism of anti-psychotic agents.

An alternative approach to the dopamine receptor is by the use of 'ligand-binding' procedures. Drugs, such as haloperidol and spiroperidol, bind to striatal tissue and with the use of radioactive labels and interactions with certain other compounds it is possible to identify the component of binding associated with the receptor (Seeman *et al.* 1976). Ligand binding is inhibited by the presence of other dopamine antagonists and the relative potencies of various neuroleptics in their interaction with the dopamine receptor, defined in this way, can be determined. The correlation between dopamine receptor antagonism and clinical potency is high (Seeman *et al.* 1976; Creese *et al.* 1976) and in this assay system the activity of the butyrophenones falls closely into line with other classes of neuroleptic drug. The receptors, which are assessed by this system, form a second and separate class of dopamine receptor, the D_2 receptor. D_2 receptors are characterized by the fact that they are not linked to stimulation of adenylate cyclase activity. D_2 receptors have a quite different specificity for agonists and antagonists from the D_1 sites. They are easily studied *in vitro* by using as radioligands potent butyrophenones, such as spiperone, which bind with nanomolar affinities (Creese *et al.* 1978; Seeman 1980).

Neuroendocrinological advances

Advances in neuroendocrinology made in the late 1960s and early 1970s provided a further means of examining dopaminergic and other neurotransmitter mechanisms in schizophrenia. The idea that symptoms referable to the nervous system and indeed those of schizophrenia may relate to endocrine effects has a long history (see Chapter 1). The direct investigation of such relationships is, of course, much more recent and has been greatly aided by the development of specific and sensitive radioimmunoassays for anterior pituitary hormones (Berson and Yalow 1968). Neuro-pharmacological studies allied with histochemical and immunofluorescence techniques have established that biogenic amines and other neurotransmitters play a critical role in the modulation of anterior pituitary hormone secretion (APHS) through an action on the hypothalamic hypophysiotrophic neurones (Fuxe and Hokfelt 1969). The tubero-infundibular dopaminergic system is situated in the medial basal hypothalamus. It has been shown that there is a close anatomical relationship between this system and the hypothalamic neurones containing releasing factors for anterior pituitary hormone secretion (Martin 1973; McNeill and Sladek 1978). Blockade of D_2 receptors is the major factor in the inhibitory effect of anti-psychotic drugs on pituitary lactotrophic cells (Muller *et al.* 1977). There is evidence to suggest that dopamine acts directly as the primary prolactin inhibiting factor (Ben-Jonathan *et al.* 1977). Prolactin secretion has been found to be elevated after neuroleptic administration in normal subjects (Kleinberg *et al.* 1971) and in schizophrenic patients. Drugs which are known to be effective neuroleptics were found to cause an elevation of prolactin levels, although with clozapine the rise was small (Meltzer *et al.* 1979). Positive relationships were demonstrated between the anti-psychotic effects of neuroleptics and the associated elevation of prolactin (Meltzer and Fang 1976; Cotes *et al.* 1978), although the associations were not strong and were only apparent at low doses of neuroleptics. This and other issues such as the time lag (Cotes *et al.* 1978) between the rapid elevation of prolactin and the slower anti-psychotic effects associated with neuroleptics suggested that clinical response was not related to dopaminergic blockade in an entirely straightforward manner.

Receptor studies

Initial studies of dopamine receptors concerned D_1 and D_2 types but other categories of dopamine receptors D_3 (Sokoloff *et al.* 1990) and D_4 and D_5 (Van Tol *et al.* 1991; Sunahara *et al.* 1991) have been characterized more recently, although their relevance for neuroleptic treatment and schizophrenia has yet to be clearly established. Although later studies of drugs with multiple actions have indicated that some of these may have some advantages over relatively pure D_2 blockers (Kane *et al.* 1988; Editorial, *Lancet* 1992) D_2 dopamine receptor blockade has remained the key feature for anti-psychotic activity. This naturally led to consideration of the possibility that dopaminergic mechanisms were disturbed in schizophrenia and indeed was one of the two main lines of evidence on which the dopamine hypotheses of schizophrenia was based, i.e. that schizophrenia is associated with excessive dopaminergic function in the central nervous system. The other main line of evidence was the fact that amphetamine and other dopamine-releasing drugs if used by non-psychotic individuals could induce a schizophrenia-like paranoid state (Connell 1958; Griffiths *et al.* 1972; Angrist *et al.* 1974). Studies of dopaminergic function in schizophrenic patients have not generally yielded evidence of excessive activity. Studies of the concentration of homovanillic acid (HVA), the major end-product of dopamine metabolism in the brain, yielded no evidence of increased dopamine turnover in schizophrenics (Bowers 1974; Post *et al.* 1975). Direct measurements of dopaminergic mechanisms have also been made in post-mortem brains of schizophrenics but results are inconsistent. Bird *et al.* (1977) reported significantly increased dopamine levels in nucleus accumbens but not in putamen, whereas Owen *et al.* (1978) reported a moderate increase in caudate nucleus but no difference between controls and schizophrenics in either the putamen or nucleus accumbens. Measurements of HVA in schizophrenic brains have produced no evidence of increased dopamine turnover (Owen *et al.* 1978; Bird *et al.* 1979) and no difference was demonstrated between schizophrenics and controls in the activity of tyrosine hydroxylase, the rate-limiting enzyme in catecholamine syntheses (Crow *et al.* 1979*a*). Overall, therefore, the studies in cerebrospinal fluid and brain of metabolites and the activities of enzymes involved in the synthesis and inactivation of dopamine did not support the dopamine hypotheses of schizophrenia. However, it had been suggested by Bowers in 1974 that the postulated disturbance in dopamine systems in schizophrenic brain might not be in the presynaptic dopamine neurone but at the level of the postsynaptic receptor. The development of high-affinity binding techniques to assess dopamine receptors (Seeman *et al.* 1976) as described above allowed this issue to be investigated. Several studies have shown that dopamine receptors identified as butyrophenone binding sites are increased in the caudate nucleus, putamen, and nucleus accumbens in schizophrenic post-mortem brain (Lee *et al.* 1978; Crow *et al.* 1979*b*; Owen *et al.* 1981). The question of whether or not these changes are related to neuroleptic medication or to the disease process is clearly central to the issue. In some of the work carried out at the Clinical Research Centre (CRC) at Northwick Park, north-west London, (Owen *et al.* 1978, 1981; Crow *et al.* 1979*b*) the changes were seen in patients who had apparently not received neuroleptic drugs for at least one year before death and similar results were found by Lee *et al.* (1978). In the work of Mackay *et al.* (1982) the brains of such neuroleptic-free patients did not show any increase in binding. These results could be less incompatible than at first they appear because in all studies the range of values in the schizophrenic group is wide and the overlap with controls substantial, but, on the other hand it is very difficult to establish beyond doubt the absence of past neuroleptic history. The CRC patients used in this work were part of the large sample of schizophrenic patients at Shenley Hospital who received extensive study from many aspects. One of the great advantages of this population was that it included groups of patients who had been treated by psychiatrists with widely differing views on the appropriate management of schizophrenia, some having orthodox views and others being opposed to the use of physical treatments. This meant that at the time this population began to receive extensive study by the CRC staff (Owens and Johnstone 1980) there were 65 patients fulfilling the St. Louis criteria (Feighner *et al.* 1972) for schizophrenia whose drug cards showed that they had never been prescribed neuroleptics. The nurses could not recall these patients every having received such drugs and this was in keeping with the treatment policy of the consultants concerned. It is always possible to question the accuracy of drug cards and, of course, the brains of relatively few of these patients became available before the receptor studies were done. Those who did die by that time were in general too incapacitated to even discuss their past treatment with the investigators. The development in the early 1980s of techniques for assessing dopamine receptors in life with positron emission (Wagner *et al.* 1983) and gamma emission (Crawley *et al.* 1986) allowed the possibility of eventual resolution of the issue of whether the receptor changes were due to the illness or its drug treatment. At present findings are conflicting (Wong *et al.* 1986; Farde *et al.* 1987, 1990) but the balance of the evidence at present is that there is no difference between schizophrenics and controls in terms of density and affinity of D_2 dopamine receptors.

The substantial technical advances of the 1970s and early 1980s allowed psychopharmacological and neuroendocrine studies and other measures of neurotransmission in schizophrenia to be conducted with an accuracy and in a detail which could hardly have been imagined in earlier decades. To a certain extent, this has been a great success because the understanding of the mode of action of anti-psychotic drugs has been a substantial advance. On the other hand, while it was hoped by at least some of the investigators involved in this work, that understanding of the mechanism of action of the drugs used to treat schizophrenia would reveal the underlying mechanism of the disorder, that hope has not been realized. It has been established beyond reasonable doubt that the principal relevant mode of action of currently available typical anti-psychotic drugs is blockade of D_2 dopamine receptors but this has not helped us to understand the mechanism which produces the clinical picture of schizophrenia.

Structural imaging

Structural imaging of the brain in life dates back to Dandy's introduction of pneumoencephalography in 1919, but the invention of computer assisted tomography by Hounsfield in 1973 represented a major advance in the investigation of the structure of the living brain. Essentially, computed tomography (CT) is a procedure in which X-ray transmission readings are taken through the head at many angles by means of a narrow beam of X-rays. From these data absorption values of the material contained within the head are calculated and presented as a series of pictures of transverse slices of the cranial contents. The system exposes the patient to no greater radiation dosage than a standard series of ordinary skull X-rays. There is no need for anaesthesia or any form of invasive procedure. It is thus possible to use normal subjects as controls in CT investigations in a way that was not acceptable with pneumoencephalography. Gawler *et al.* (1975) described the findings in the normal brain and the range of structures identifiable by early CT scans. Within the cerebral substance, the thalami, the heads of the caudate nuclei, the internal capsule and the optic radiations were generally identifiable and clear representations of both the lateral and third ventricles could be obtained. A number of pathological processes are readily visualized including tumours, abscesses, haematomas, and local cerebral oedema.

Computed tomography in schizophrenia

My colleagues and I working at the Clinical Research Centre, Northwick Park, conducted the first CT scan study comparing the brains of schizophrenic patients with those of normal controls. (Johnstone *et al.* 1976, 1978*a*). This study showed that lateral ventricular area was increased in a group of chronically institutionalized schizophrenic patients in comparison with an age matched group of normal controls (see Fig. 2.1). Numerous

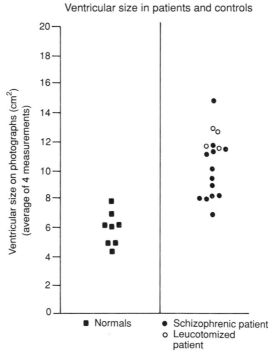

Fig. 2–1 Lateral ventricular area assessed from computerized axial tomographs in the chronic schizophrenics and age-matched controls in the initial CT scan study (Johnstone *et al.* 1976, 1978*a*).

studies of lateral ventricular size have been carried out subsequently using CT and later, magnetic resonance imaging. Many, although not all, have confirmed the findings (Owens *et al.* 1985; Johnstone *et al.* 1989*a*), and results of this kind have been extensively reviewed (Weinberger *et al.* 1983; Gattaz *et al.* 1991).

Our interest in imaging studies developed almost by chance. Crow and Mitchell (1975) had demonstrated that a subgroup of patients with chronic schizophrenia were disorientated with regard to their own age and Tim Crow suggested that this result could be interpreted as showing that in some schizophrenic patients the development of schizophrenia was associated with the development of defective learning capacity. This work had been done in Scotland but once the Division of Psychiatry at the Clinical Research Centre was established the finding was further explored in the long-stay patients at Shenley Hospital (Stevens *et al.* 1978). When I was examining these patients in connection with that study, it was evident to me that although, at least in some cases, there was a detailed account of their illness at the time of admission, the notes in subsequent years were often very limited and many of the patients could no longer give any real account of their complaints or history. It seemed to me that it was possible that in these very impaired, age disorientated patients some additional dementing process could have developed separately from the condition with which they were initially admitted. Furthermore, before accepting the idea that development of learning capacity was a feature of schizophrenia *per se* it would be appropriate to investigate these patients for known causes of pre-senile dementia. Subsequently, CT scans were carried out on some of the Shenley patients in the neurosurgical unit at the Atkinson Morley Hospital and were reported as showing cerebral atrophy. It was in the light of this result that our initial comparison of lateral ventricular size and a battery of psychological tests between groups of age disorientated schizophrenics, non-age disorientated schizophrenics, and normal controls matched for age and occupational level was conducted (all subjects were male). It had initially been intended to include a group of patients receiving long-term institutional care for physical illness and the psychological tests were carried out (Johnstone *et al.* 1978*a*) on patients from the Royal Home and Hospital for Incurables in Putney but these frail incapacitated patients could not lie comfortably in the CT scanner for more than a few moments. The relatively prolonged scanning time required in 1975 proved impossible for them. In summary, this study showed that in comparison with the normal control group the schizophrenic patients had significantly (P <0.01) increased lateral ventricular size and that in comparison with both the normal control group and the group institutionalized because of physical illness the schizophrenics showed substantial impairments on intellectual testing. The differences in ventricular size between schizophrenic patients and normal controls remained significant after the four patients who had been leucotomized had been excluded. Within the non-leucotomized schizophrenic group ventricular size was significantly associated with intellectual impairment (P <0.01). Past physical treatment had been variable in these patients and there was no evidence to suggest that these treatments had caused the ventricular enlargement (see Table 2.1) but, of course, this small and selected sample did not allow adequate exploration of this issue.

The demonstration that not only were the lateral ventricles of the schizophrenic subjects larger than those of controls but that the cognitive impairments of the schizophrenic patients were significantly associated with ventricular enlargement renewed interest in the cognitive changes in schizophrenia (Kendell 1986). Poor performance on cognitive tests in schizophrenia had long been noted. Since E. Bleuler's early writings, however, the view that in spite of the poor performance, the cognitive abilities of schizophrenic patients did not decline had held sway. It was believed that the patients did not do the tests, did not seem to know their own age, their date of birth or occasionally even their own name because of lack of volition rather than lack of ability. The idea was that through lack of interest and drive the patients did not try to do the tests but that if this veil of apathy could be lifted the patients' abilities lay unimpaired behind it. Once the poor performance could be related to structural changes the idea of preserved abilities behind a veil became much less credible and extensive studies of cognitive inmpairments in schizophrenic patients since that time have shown that in a proportion of patients with schizophrenia, cognitive impairments are definite and may be severe and crippling (Frith 1987, 1992; Nelson *et al.* 1990; McKenna *et al.* 1990; Tamlyn *et al.* 1992; Shallice *et al.* 1991).

It is important to bear in mind that these impairments occur only in a

Table 2–1 *Relationship between ventricular/brain ratio (VBR) and history of physical treatment in initial CT study of Schizophrenia (Johnstone et al. 1976, 1978a). Leucotomized cases omitted*

	Mean ventricular size VBR		
	History of treatment (No. of cases)	*No history of treatment (No. of cases)*	*Probability*
ECT	9.9	10.0	
	(6)	(7)	NS
Neuroleptics	9.3	11.3	
	(9)	(4)	NS
Insulin comas	8.5	11.2	
	(6)	(7)	<0.05

proportion of patients with schizophrenia. The heterogeneity of schizophrenia has been discussed so frequently (Lindenmayer and Kay 1992) that the phrase has become something of a cliché but the representativeness, or otherwise, of samples of schizophrenic patients used in investigations, such as imaging studies, is an important issue. Certainly the sample of 17 schizophrenic patients successfully scanned in the original CT scan project (Johnstone *et al.* 1976, 1978*a*) were far from typical of the generality of patients with schizophrenia. They were selected from a group of patients who had an illness of such severity that they had required continuous inpatient care for at least 20 years. Hospital statistics concerning patients with a diagnosis of schizophrenia admitted in the same decade as most of this group suggest that in only about 40 per cent of cases did the illness run this deteriorating course (Harris and Norris 1955). Furthermore, they were not randomly selected from the population of long-stay inpatient schizophrenics in the wards from which they came. The selection of subjects for the investigation was dependent upon their willingness to co-operate with transfer to an unfamiliar environment and co-operate at least to some extent with various procedures. It might be argued that such docility would correlate with a degree of cognitive impairment and it was evident that in order to pursue the findings of this study it would be necessary to carry out further investigations. The results of this study and of the earlier pneumoencephalographic work of Haug (1962), Huber (1964), and Asano (1967) suggested that among patients with schizophrenia where the illness ran a deteriorating course there was a group where the disease was associated with increased ventricular size and impaired intellectual capacity. It seemed to those involved in the study at that time that the matter of whether the increase in ventricular size was a factor which predisposes towards a deteriorating course or whether it was a direct result of the disease process was an important question but one that could not be answered on the basis of the data then available. Since that time evidence has been put forward (Lewis 1989) to suggest the additional possibility that the enlarged ventricles pre-date the onset of the schizophrenic illness and are evidence of a developmental abnormality which underlies the condition. Other issues raised by the early findings were the extent to which ventricular enlargement would be found in the generality of schizophrenic patients and indeed in first episode cases, the relevance of physical treatments and perhaps the circumstances of institutional care for the enlargement, the nature of the clinical correlates of the enlargement, and lastly and arguably most importantly, the nature of the cellular change underlying this appearance. Further studies have been carried out to explore these issues but only some of them have been resolved. The detailed information available about the 17 schizophrenic patients in the first CT scan study (Johnstone *et al.* 1976, 1978*b*) continues to be of some relevance to current controversies in this area. There has been much comment (Castle and Murray 1991; Lewis 1989) in support of the view that at least some schizophrenic patients, particularly those whose illness has run a deteriorating course, who are male, and who have ventricular enlargement, have never functioned at a normal level and have shown cognitive and perhaps other abnormalities in childhood. This may well be so and indeed the work carried out in the early 1990s by my colleagues and me (Done *et al.* 1991) on the National Child Development Study could be interpreted in this way, but perusal of the biographical details of the patients in the 1976 study does not support this view. There can be no doubt that the illness in these male patients has run a malignant course and because in this study (unlike most of those which followed it) there is almost no overlap in ventricular size between schizophrenics and controls, they unquestionably have ventricular enlargement. The evidence that we have does not suggest that their pre-morbid function was universally poor (see Table 2.2). Cases 15 and 18 came from working class homes from which a scholarship to a grammar school and certainly a career as a local government clerk were considerable achievements. The relatives of case 7 stated that in the 1930s he earned over £1000 per annum as a commercial artist, which was a very high salary at that time. Case 6 was a principal violinist in Geraldo's Dance Band, one of the most famous 1930s dance orchestras. We were told that he toured the Astoria ballrooms throughout Britain in this capacity for some years and enjoyed considerable financial success.

Anecdotes can be very appealing but evidence based on them is often misleading and in order to study representative samples of schizophrenic patients and consider the issues arising from the CT scan study my colleagues and I began a series of large studies documenting and examining complete cohorts of schizophrenic and other patients from which we would be able to select representative groups in order to examine particular questions in a better controlled CT study. The questions that we wished to ask at that time were:

1. Is schizophrenia indeed associated with lateral ventricular enlargement?

2. Is that enlargement diagnosis specific?

3. Is it the result of physical methods of treatment?

4. When present, what are its correlates?

It was evident that our access to the large population of schizophrenic inpatients in Shenley Hospital provided us with unusual opportunities to examine these issues. As noted earlier this population included groups of patients who had been treated by psychiatrists with very different views on physical treatment. The hospital had provided all psychiatric care for patients from the London boroughs of Brent and Harrow. Although these boroughs are now somewhat different in social composition this was much less so in the 1940s, 1950s, and 1960s. The consultant in charge of wards for patients from Brent had orthodox views on physical treatments and patients under his care were given these in a wide range of doses. The consultant on the Harrow side was evidently of the view that hospitals were places of asylum and that conventional behaviour should not be imposed upon patients by means of physical treatment. He avoided the use of physical treatment wherever possible. We were able to match pairs of patients who had and had not had physical treatments for age, sex, and length of illness. In order to take full advantage of this situation the entire inpatient population (1227 cases) was surveyed. The St Louis criteria (Feighner *et al.* 1972) for schizophrenia were applied to the casenotes of the 635 patients with a casenote diagnosis of schizophrenia who had been in hospital continuously for one year or more. Of these, 524 patients fulfilled the criteria and the 510 who survived to participate were examined in terms of their mental state, cognitive functioning, neurological status, and behavioural performance. These findings were related to historical information including details of past physical treatment received (Owens and Johnstone 1980). From this database it was possible to select particular groups of patients to examine the clinical correlates of larger ventricular size and the effects of physical treatment (Owens *et al.* 1985). The pneumencephalographic study of Haug (1962) indicated that increased ventricular size in schizophrenia was associated with global deterioration of function. In the initial CT study (Johnstone *et al.* 1976), increased ventricular/brain ratio (VBR) was significantly associated with poor cognitive performance. In the survey as a whole (Owens and Johnstone 1980), indices of deterioration and defect as assessed by negative features, neurological signs, and behavioural performance were associated with poor cognitive performance. Positive features were not associated with any indices of deterioration. In the light of these findings it was postulated (Crow *et al.* 1979*b*, 1982) that structural brain changes are more likely to be associated with negative or defect symptoms. Patients with and without a defect state according to defined criteria were therefore compared in the second CT study (Owens *et al.* 1985, Johnstone *et al.* 1989*a*). Those with and without defect were matched on each of the following variables: age, sex, length of illness, past educational record, gross neurological (excluding extrapyramidal) signs, past insulin treatment, past electroconvulsive therapy (ECT) treatment, and past neuroleptic treatment. In order to investigate the role of physical treatment samples who had received no ECT, insulin or neuroleptic treatment were compared with samples matched for age, sex, and duration of illness who had been heavily treated by these methods. Further groups included for examination of clinical correlates consisted of patients with a university education with and without current evidence of cognitive impairment and

Table 2-2 Brief biographical details of schizophrenics in original CT study (Johnstone et al. 1976, 1978a)

Case no.	Age	Duration of hospitalization (yrs)	Previous occupation	Additional biographical details
1	64	39	Wireless engineer	Nil
2	42	24	Warehouse assistant	Steadily employed for 4 years
3	66	41	Labourer	Nil
4	53	32	Naval rating	Entered Navy as boy, good performance until ill
5	66	42	Clerk	Nil
6	63	39	Violinist	Highly successful in famous dance band
7	52	23	Commercial artist	Highly successful artist in film studios
8	47	25	Labourer	Poor school performance
9	69	38	Clerk	Scholarship to grammar school, always first in class
10	66	40	Salesman	Completed 5-year apprenticeship in his trade

Table 2-2 cont.

Case no.	Age	Duration of hospitalization (yrs)	Previous occupation	Additional biographical details
11	54	24	Upholsterer	Top stream at school
12	63	42	Dining car attendant	Top stream at school
13	70	32	Bus conductor	Good work record; amateur violinist
14	47	20	Labourer	Said to do well at school
15	53	28	Clerk	Scholarship to grammar school, successful local government clerk
16	64	28	Coalman	Nil
17	54	29	Army driver	Lathe operator before army service
18	46	27	RAF Serviceman	Scholarship to grammar school

samples of patients whose initial illness had been classed as catatonic (Wing *et al.* 1974) as these seemed to form a subgroup whose impairments were particularly severe.

These various selected samples of patients with chronic schizophrenia came to a total of 112 individuals. The questions listed above concerning physical treatments and clinical correlates could be examined within this population. However, in order to examine the first and second questions listed we required control groups. To consider the issue of whether or not schizophrenia is associated with lateral ventricular enlargement we required to extend our schizophrenic sample beyond those requiring long-term institutional care and we required a suitable non-schizophrenic population for comparison. To examine, the issue of diagnostic specificity we needed to include patients who were not suffering from schizophrenia but who had required long-term inpatient care. Altogether the study concerned six groups of patients:

1. The selected groups of schizophrenic patients receiving long-term inpatient care.

2. Matched cases selected from the 120 patients discharged from Shenley between 1970 and 1975 who fulfilled the St. Louis criteria (Feighner *et al.* 1972) for schizophrenia but never returned to long-term inpatient care.

3. Matched cases selected from the 29 of the 1227 Shenley inpatients at the time of the survey who fulfilled operational criteria for manic-depressive illness and had been receiving continuous inpatient care for at least one year.

4. Manic depressive outpatients selected from those attending the clincs of the participating clinicians.

5. Patients with first psychotic episodes fulfilling the PSE/CATEGO (Wing *et al.* 1974) criteria for schizophrenia.

6. Neurotic outpatients attending the outpatient clinics of the participating clinicians and fulfilling the St. Louis (Feighner *et al.* 1972) criteria for anxiety neurosis or undiagnosed psychiatric illness.

The neurotic patients were chosen as a control group, and represented the best available alternative rather than an ideal choice. The choice of the best control group for studies of this kind is not easy and difficulties relating to control groups have been widely discussed. Indeed, it has been suggested that the finding of increased ventricular size in schizophrenics may be spurious and due to the nature of the controls (Smith and Iacono 1986). This analysis omitted the findings of the investigators at the Clinical Research Centre (CRC) and has been disputed (Owen and Lewis 1986) but the difficulties of selecting suitable controls remain. Diverse groups have been used including relatives of patients with Huntington's chorea (Weinberger *et al.* 1979), scans reported as normal by radiology departments (Andreasen *et al.* 1982), road accident victims (Nasrallah *et al.* 1982), and normal volunteers largely obtained from hospital staff (Jernigan *et al.* 1982). There are problems with all such groups. Normal asymptomatic volunteers would be ideal if a reliable and detailed history of possible central nervous system disease, alcohol and drug intake, and family history of psychosis could be taken and if volunteers could be matched with the experimental sample for age and other factors, such as social and academic background, which may be relevant. Such samples are hard to find and it was considered that the advantage of the detailed personal and family information, and the lifetime history of drug and alcohol intake available on the neurotic patients was such that they were the best control group available to us. Patients known to have problems relating to alcohol or drug use were not included. Alcohol intake, which may be relevant (Ron *et al.* 1982) was described as low but many of these patients had a long duration of psychotropic drug prescription, mainly benzodiazepines and anti-depressants. It has been suggested (Lader *et al.* 1984) that benzodiazepine ingestion is associated with the development of ventricular enlargement. It could well be argued that the use of a control group of neurotic patients many of whom had received benzodiazepines may have minimized the extent of the ventricular enlargement in the other groups. This may be so, but, with age taken into account, the patients with chronic schizophrenia had significantly larger ventricles than the neurotic patients and the mean VBR of the schizophrenic groups was significantly greater (P < 0.02) than that of the non-schizophrenic groups taken together (see Fig. 2.2).

There was, however, a much greater overlap between the measurements in the schizophrenic and control samples than was found in the earlier study. Examination of the findings in the groups of schizophrenic patients matched from the point of view of treatment, showed no differences and indeed did not show even any slight trend which would have suggested a role for physical treatments in the production of the ventricular enlargement (see Table 2.3). It was pleasing that these samples were able to provide this clear result because opportunities for examining the role of physical treatments in relation to structural changes are limited and are not likely to become less so. By contrast, the findings relating to clinical correlates were somewhat disappointing. Our carefully selected groups did not reveal a clear relationship with the defect state (defined in terms of cognitive impairment and negative features), although increased ventricular size was related to impaired social behaviour, inactivity and the presence of abnormal involuntary movements.

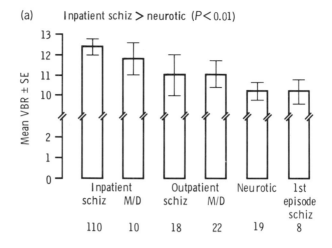

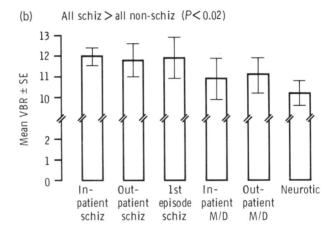

Fig. 2–2. (a) VBRs in matched groups of schizophrenic patients and controls with other psychiatric disorders.
(b) VBRs in matched groups of schizophrenic patients and controls with other psychiatric disorders corrected for age differences.

At the time that this study was designed we were influenced by the view (Crow 1980) that schizophrenia involved two separate processes, a structural one demonstrated by imaging studies, and a neurochemical one demonstrated by the responsiveness of some symptoms to neuroleptic medication. The concept we held at that time was that positive symptoms (e.g. delusions and hallucinations) are associated with a neurochemical disturbance which is at least potentially reversible and responsive to

Table 2–3 *Comparison of VBRs In schizophrenic cases matched for exposure/ no exposure to physical treatments (Owens et al. 1985)*

Comparison group	No. of cases	VBR (mean ±SD)	Significance using paired tests
No physical treatments vs.	9	13.1 ± 3.7	NS
Heavy physical treatment	7	11.5 ± 2.7	
No insulin vs.	8	13.4 ± 2.0	NS
*Much insulin (matched for ECT and neuroleptics)	8	11.4 ± 4.8	
No ECT vs.	8	12.6 ± 2.1	NS
*Much ECT (matched for insulin and neuroleptics)	8	13.0 ± 3.3	
No neuroleptics vs.	8	14.5 ± 4.0	NS
*Much neuroleptic (matched for insulin and ECT)	8	13.0 ± 3.5	

* Definition of 'much' insulin, ECT, and neuroleptic, given in Owens *et al.* (1985).

neuroleptic drugs, whereas negative symptoms (e.g. affective flattening and poverty of speech) are related to structural, possibly irreversible, changes in the brain. If this were so we would have expected to see clear relationships with negative or defect symptoms and our findings in this respect were tentative rather than definite. One very clear result from this study was that whatever may be the group finding there are some patients who have consistently for many years shown profound negative features who have no evidence of ventricular enlargement or other structural abnormality. One of the questions that we initially posed (see above) had been answered before the study was completed. It was evident (Ron *et al.* 1982; Lader *et al.* 1984) that the enlargement is not diagnosis-specific. We were able to demonstrate, however, that lateral ventricular enlargement is associated at least to some degree with the generality of schizophrenia and we could find no evidence to suggest that this enlargement is a result of physical treatment. Relatively few clinical correlates were found, although the significant relationships which were found concerned inactivity and social impairments. The issue of the clinical correlates of ventricular enlargement has not been greatly illuminated by subsequent studies, although they tend to be measures of poorer outcome in some sense (for a review see Owens 1992). Other major issues raised by the finding of lateral ventricular enlargement in schizophrenia were not addressed by the first analysis of these scans. These concern; (a) the nature of the cellular change underlying the loss of brain substance implied by increased ventricular size; and (b) the point in the course of the disease at which the structural changes develop. These issues were addressed by subsequent studies and analyses.

Magnetic resonance imaging

Nuclear magnetic resonance imaging (known as NMR or MRI) became available in the early 1980s. Early work conducted by our collaborators at the Hammersmith Hospital concerned multiple sclerosis (Young *et al.* 1981) and the group as a whole was impressed with the idea that in addition to displaying structural changes in the brain with greater definition than was possible with CT, MRI had the potential of displaying pathological processes unseen by CT. In the late 1970s, our studies had suggested the possibility that there was a cytopathic affect in the cerebrospinal fluid of some schizophrenic patients. We were consistently unable to replicate this finding (Taylor *et al.* 1982), but for a time remained somewhat influenced by the idea that acute schizophrenia might be associated with some kind of acute disease process in the brain. We were able to confirm in a post-mortem study (Brown *et al.* 1986) the reduction in brain substance implied by the increased lateral ventricular size found in the CT studies (Johnstone *et al.* 1976; Owens *et al.* 1985). We considered it possible that this cell loss, or shrinkage, might result from a pathological process associated with periventricular swelling or inflamation in the acute phase and that this process might be demonstrable by MRI. A few acute untreated first episode schizophrenic patients were examined with MRI. The radiologists considered that some of the spin echo films showed an unusual increase in the light area at the anterolateral angles of the ventricles and that this could reflect the type of pathological process that we had hypothesized.

We therefore compared the periventricular appearances on MRI of four groups of young schizophrenic patients with age-matched controls (Johnstone *et al.* 1986a). Three of the groups of schizophrenics had become ill about two years previously and had participated in the Northwick Park Study of First Episodes of Schizophrenia (Johnstone *et al.* 1986b). We examined those of:(1) good pre-morbid function with a good outcome at two years;(2) good pre-morbid function with a poor outcome at two years;(3) poor pre-morbid function and poor outcome. A fourth group consisted of neuroleptic-free patients with first schizophrenic episodes. All patients and controls were in their early twenties and almost all were male. The principal comparison was between normal controls and patients with untreated first schizophrenic episodes. If differences were found it would be important to know if the abnormalities persisted beyond the first episode and whether or not such persistence was associated with the nature of the outcome of the episode. The radiologists demonstrated the relevant appearances on the scans to the clinicians involved and all five investigators blindly graded the appearances in every subject. The inter-rater reliability was high (Kendal's $W = 0.53$, $P = < 0.00001$) and no individual rater deviated significantly from the remainder. Ratings from all investigators were therefore summed and the cases were ranked in terms of this figure: The results are shown in Fig. 2.3.

There were no significant differences between any of the groups and no difference between all schizophrenics and controls. Some individuals with a high rank in terms of numbers of investigators rating them as definitely abnormal were found in all groups including the control sample. Our conclusions at the time were that the appearance of an increased light area at the anterolateral angles of the ventricles is not related to the nature of an early schizophrenic episode or indeed to the diagnosis of schizophrenia. Further experience with MRI has clearly demonstrated that this appearance of increased light at the angles of the ventricles occurs quite often and is of no known pathological significance. This

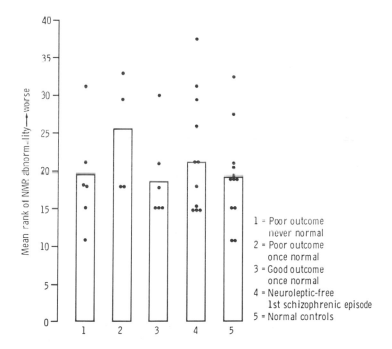

Fig. 2–3. NMR scans of schizophrenics and normal controls in terms of putative abnormality.

study was conducted with exceptional care. The patients were very closely matched and as many were drawn from a multi-centre study (Johnstone *et al.* 1986*b*) the investigation involved the transport of some quite disturbed people over substantial distances. Considerable patience was required to obtain the co-operation of drug-free, young schizophrenics, with the prolonged scanning procedure involved in MRI in the early 1980s. The investigators were much aware that they had the advantage of using a new technique available to few. The findings made it clear that a new and powerful technique and ideal patient samples are not useful if the limits of the normal appearances using that technique are not really known.

Later analyses of the CT study

After the comparison of the CT scans of the chronic schizophrenics and other groups had been completed more detailed measurements of the scans were made and these were related to the results of the extensive psychological assessments made on the schizophrenics at the time of the scans (Johnstone *et al.* 1989*a*). All measurements showed a consistent trend towards a reduction in brain substance and an increase in the brain spaces in the schizophrenic patients as compared with others, the difference varying between measurements from 3 per cent to 17 per cent. Of the seven psychological tests conducted in the schizophrenic patients only memory for famous names in the distant past (a test for memory of events 20–30 years previously) showed significant associations with ventricular size. This was interpreted as suggesting that at least in some cases ventricular enlargement and its psychological sequelae occur relatively early in the disease process. As the famous personalities (distant) test referred to a time preceding the onset of the illness in some patients particularly those with a relatively late onset, it seemed appropriate to subdivide the sample by age of onset—as had been done previously in connection with developmental (Jakob and Beckmann 1986) and neurochemical (Mackay *et al.* 1982) studies of schizophrenia. This strategy revealed that a range of clinical and psychological functions are significantly more abnormal in those with an early age of onset than in those where the onset was later. Early onset cases also performed less well academically and occupationally before illness onset. Within the early onset group some significant correlations between cognitive function and brain area were seen. The findings were interpreted as suggesting that at least some of the structural changes in schizophrenia arise at a time when the brain is still developing. The differences between the early and late onset cases could be considered to support the view that there is more than one pathway to the development of schizophrenia.

Further MRI work

The last completed structural imaging study from the Division of Psychiatry, Clinical Research Centre, was an MRI study of temporal lobe structure (Johnstone *et al*. 1989*b*). We had concluded from the findings of the earlier imaging studies that it was important to be involved in post-mortem studies of schizophrenic brains. Our first finding in that area concerned brain weight (Brown *et al*. 1986). The implication from the imaging studies is that the ventricles are larger because the brain substance is less. Without confirmation of this reduction of brain substance at post-mortem it could reasonably have been concluded that technical and other difficulties with imaging studies had led to incorrect conclusions. To the relief of at least some investigators direct support of the structural changes shown by imaging studies was provided by post-mortem studies of brain weight and ventricular size (Brown *et al*. 1986). This work showed that the greatest differences lay in the temporal lobe and a later investigation comparing the brains of schizophrenics and normal controls (Crow *et al*. 1988) showed that the increased size of the lateral ventricles in the schizophrenics became increasingly prominent posteriorly and was greatest in the temporal horn where there was an increase of 80 per cent. The temporal horn of the lateral ventricles is not well visualized on CT but can be seen on MRI scans. A comparison of the temporal lobes and the temporal horns of the lateral ventricles was therefore conducted between patients with schizophrenia, patients with affective psychosis, and normal controls. Differences were confined to male subjects but temporal horn was significantly reduced in schizophrenics as compared with the other two groups. In the post-mortem study the difference was 80 per cent but in this study where the patients were 30 to 40 years younger than those in the post-mortem investigation the difference was 34 per cent. Consideration of the temporal lobe as a whole revealed a significant diagnosis by side interaction—the area being less on the left than on the right side in patients with schizophrenia, in contrast to the findings in the two other groups.

The findings are relevant to the important question of whether or not the structural changes in the brain are progressive, but they may be interpreted in more than one way. On one hand, comparison of the rather modest changes in temporal horn area in the present study with the more striking findings in our post-mortem study (Crow *et al*. 1988) suggests if the patients are comparable then there is an element of progression. On the other hand, the fact that there are differences, albeit small ones, in temporal lobe area between young schizophrenic patients and the comparison groups suggests that some of this change may be present early, that is that it represents developmental arrest rather than neuronal degeneration.

Interpretation of imaging studies in schizophrenia

Seventeen years after our first admittedly small and crude imaging study (Johnstone *et al.* 1976) it is gratifying to find that there has been general support for the results from many CT, MRI, and post-mortem studies of much more sophisticated methodology, and using much larger samples and many types of controls. In the 1976 study, assessable scans were obtained from only 17 patients and initially the measurements were derived by tracing the brain and ventricular outlines by hand on to millimetre-squared tracing paper. However, the findings have proved more robust than those of some of our much larger and more meticulous studies. While the finding of structural changes has received widespread support and has led to some very valuable psychological and post-mortem studies as well as other imaging studies it is perhaps rather disappointing that some central questions remain unresolved. These are principally the nature of the cellular change, the cause of this change, and whether or not it progresses. The balance of the evidence is probably that it does not progress but studies in this area are generally very small (Nasrallah *et al.* 1986; Illowsky *et al.* 1988) and the technical difficulties have been already described (Owens 1992). The developmental versus degenerative hypothesis has received substantial study and perhaps even more heated discussion. It may well be that there is truth in both arguments and that schizophrenia is heterogeneous in its causation as well as in its manifestation but no such conclusion could be drawn from the imaging studies alone. Perfect design is difficult to achieve in imaging studies and less than ideal control groups have been a feature of our own investigations (Owens *et al.* 1985; Johnstone *et al.* 1989*b*) as well as those of many others. These restrict the interpretation of the results and the use to which even large data sets can be put. An illustration of this concerns the interesting finding of Andreasen *et al.* (1990) where a CT study of ventricular size shows a significant diagnosis × gender interaction. In their sample the major component of difference between schizophrenics and controls could be accounted for by differences in the males alone. Andreasen *et al.* (1990) express concern about the suitability of their control group in this study but the problems which we had in recruiting female subjects, especially female controls, for some of the projects (Johnstone *et al.* 1976, 1986*a*, 1989*b*) would make it difficult for us to examine this important issue in our own samples.

3

Pharmacological studies

Chlorpromazine was introduced into psychiatric practice on an empirical basis in 1952 by Delay and Deniker. Although initially psychiatrists were slow to accept that this drug was an active anti-psychotic agent and not simply a super-sedative, trials conducted in the 1960s, especially the NIMH Psychopharmacology Service Center Study published in 1964, demonstrated the anti-schizophrenic activity of phenothiazines. While initially the mode of action of neuroleptics was obscure, their ability to induce Parkinsonian-like features, the work of Hornykiewicz (1973) relating Parkinsonism to depletion of dopamine from the basal ganglia, the selective effects of neuroleptic drugs on central dopamine turnover (Carlsson and Lindqvist 1963), and the fact that the drugs are able to reverse amphetamine-induced abnormal behaviours that are dependent on central dopamine release (Randrup and Munkvad 1965) pointed to the relevance of dopaminergic mechanisms. The development of *in vitro* assay systems for dopamine receptors and the advances in radioimmunoassay, allowing accurate measurement of drug levels and of levels of anterior pituitary hormones, greatly enhanced the possibilities of examining indices of dopaminergic blockade in relation to neuroleptic assessment and to testing aspects of the 'dopamine hypothesis'. Much work was done but it was largely laboratory-based (Miller *et al.* 1974; Seeman *et al.* 1976; Burt *et al.* 1977).

The isomers of flupenthixol study

The first clinical study of anti-psychotic agents conducted at the Clinical Research Centre (CRC) (Johnstone *et al.* 1978*b* was therefore presented in some settings as a test of the dopamine hypothesis as it concerns living patients who have schizophrenia. (Johnstone 1978). The basis of this study was the fact that using the dopamine-sensitive adenylate cyclase assay Miller *et al.* (1974) demonstrated that certain thiaxanthene compounds exhibit stereoisomerism, the blockade of dopamine receptors being selectively associated with one of the two isomers. An example of this is flupenthixol of which the standard oral preparation consists of a racemic mixture of two isomers *cis* and *trans*. Only the *cis*-isomer possesses significant activity in blocking dopamine receptors (Miller *et al.*

1974; Enna *et al.* 1976). A clinical trial of the two isomers was therefore conducted. The plan of the study was as follows: 45 patients with acute untreated schizophrenic symptoms were blindly allocated to one of three treatment groups each consisting of 15 patients. One group received *cis*-flupenthixol, one *trans*-flupenthixol, and the third identical placebo. With a view to preventing the emergence of Parkinsonian side-effects from revealing the allocation of the medication all patients were given orphenadrine 50 mg three times a day throughout the four weeks of the study. Because the patients were acutely ill and at least one-third were going to be receiving entirely inactive medication the possibility of giving chlorpromazine in single doses for distress or behavioural disturbance was allowed. A count of these was kept and this could be used as an additional dependent variable. This possibility was allowed in all of the acute inpatient treatment trials that we later conducted, but, in fact, as in this study, very little of this 'escape' medication was required and there were no major difficulties in safely caring for very floridly psychotic patients in placebo-controlled trials. Indeed, in the 15 years in which I conducted trials at the CRC, we did not have a single suicide in the trial inpatients in spite of the large numbers involved. Comparable facilities nearby treating similar patients with standard methods were less fortunate. In this trial, clinical ratings were done weekly and on the same day blood was removed for the assessment of drug levels, anterior pituitary hormones, and platelet monoamine oxidase (MAO), and psychophysiological measures were carried out.

The rationale behind this was that in a placebo-controlled trial of psychotic illness where a biological variable is being serially assessed there is the possibility of separating the effects upon that variable of change in the illness from those of treatment of the illness. While it is expected that much of the change will be a treatment effect, no matter how severely psychotic the patients, there are likely to be some who will show substantial improvements or even resolution of their symptoms despite being on placebo. Such cases occurred in all of the CRC studies. Similarly, some patients will show little or no response to a treatment which is of general efficacy. A placebo-controlled trial, therefore, in theory offers ideal circumstances for separating the effects of a disease from those of its treatment. This general plan was therefore operated in relation to all of the placebo-controlled trials although, of course, the biological variables varied. In practice, this strategy yielded disappointingly few positive findings of importance although the negative ones quite often made useful contributions. This relative lack of success does not of course mean that the strategy was flawed, most of the biological markers that we used, e.g. platelet MAO, and psychophysiological variables, have been shown to be less specific or less relevant than was thought at one time. In the comparison of the isomers of flupenthixol versus placebo all patients showed a significant ($P<0.05$) tendency to improve but this was significantly greater in the patients on *cis*-flupenthixol, the results in the placebo and *trans*-flupenthixol groups being closely similar (see Fig. 3.1).

This result is consistent with the dopamine blockade hypothesis and excludes various alternative mechanisms. Although it does not rule out serotonin receptor antagonism (the *cis*-isomer being significantly more effective as a serotonin antagonist) this was thought unlikely to be the mechanism of therapeutic effect because there is little relationship between clinical efficacy and the serotonin antagonist activities of a range of psychotropic drugs (Bennet and Snyder 1975). The possible involvement of serotonin mechanisms in the efficacy of some anti-psychotic agents is a more 'fashionable' concept now (Johnstone 1991) than it was in 1978 and it may be that we would have interpreted this result differently had we been looking at it for the first time in the 1990s. In 1978 our interpretation was that dopamine receptor blockade was the only pharmacological action which explained the stereoisomerism of the anti-psychotic effect of flupenthixol. In this trial some selectivity of the antipsychotic effect for particular symptoms appeared to be demonstrated (see Fig. 3.2).

At the semi-structured interviews used (Krawiecka *et al.* 1977) positive symptoms showed a significantly better response to *cis*-flupenthixol than to the other treatments (Fig. 3.2). Negative symptoms were initially less severe and thus had less opportunity to improve than positive symptoms but *cis*-flupenthixol had a negligible effect on them. This conflicts with earlier findings (e.g. Goldberg *et al.* 1965) which suggested that phenothiazines

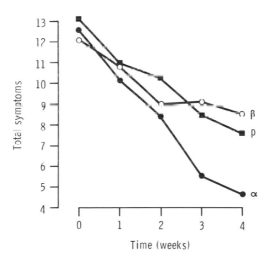

Fig. 3–1. The effect on total symptom scores using the Krawiecka (1977) scale of the α (*cis*)- and β (*trans*)- isomers of flupenthixol vs. placebo (p) in schizophrenic patients (n = 45).

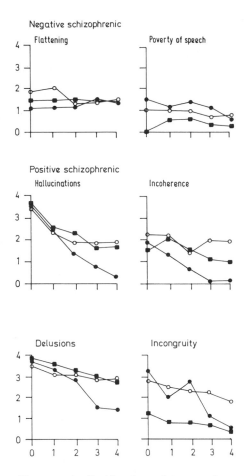

Fig. 3–2. The effect on individual positive and negative symptoms of schizophrenia using the Krawiecka (1977) scale of the α (*cis*)- and β (*trans*)- isomers of flupenthixol vs. placebo. ●, α- flupenthixol; ○, β- flupenthixol; ■, placebo.

had beneficial effects upon a wide range of schizophrenic symptoms. In a more recent review on the topic Pogue-Geile and Zubin (1988) point out that neuroleptics have been reported as improving (Goldberg *et al*. 1965; Meltzer 1985), having no effect upon (Johnstone *et al*. 1978*b*; Angrist *et al*. 1980), and exacerbating (Marder *et al*. 1984; Kane and Rifkin 1985; Hogarty *et al*. 1988) negative symptoms. They conclude that negative symptoms are probably not overwhelmingly affected by current pharmacological methods and rightly state that this is an important area which needs further research.

The flupenthixol procyclidine study

The next treatment trial which was conducted in the Division of Psychiatry, CRC, was designed in part to give a wide range of dosages of neuroleptic in order that relationships between plasma levels of neuroleptic and prolactin levels and clinical assessments could be satisfactorily examined (Johnstone *et al*. 1983). In a series of 36 patients with acute schizophrenia, flupenthixol dosage was blindly adjusted (patients being randomly and blindly allocated to identical preparations containing 1 mg, 2 mg, and 4 mg flupenthixol) to give a fixed level of sedation. After 10 days, procyclidine and placebo were randomly and blindly added to the drug regimes. The patients receiving procyclidine experienced more positive schizophrenic symptoms than those on placebo (see Fig. 3.3)

Similarly, extra-pyramidal features were less severe in patients on procyclidine. Blood levels of prolactin and flupenthixol were not significantly affected by the addition of procyclidine. There was no significant association between clinical and laboratory measures with the exception that a curvilinear relationship was demonstrated between flupenthixol levels and anti-psychotic and extra-pyramidal effects. This relationship was thought probably to be due to the fact that the design of the study meant that patients resistant to the effects of neuroleptic medication are likely to be given the highest doses. The deterioration in positive symptoms associated with the administration of procyclidine supported the similar earlier findings of Haase (1962) and Singh and Kay (1975). Pharmacokinetic effects could have accounted for the results of those studies but clearly were not the explanation for the findings of our study as blood levels of flupenthixol and of prolactin were not affected by the administration of procyclidine. This result was interpreted as suggesting either that the site of the anti-psychotic effect of neuroleptics may not be as restricted or that the cholinergic-dopaminergic interaction and its relevance to the anti-psychotic effect may not be as straightforward as was previously believed. We did not directly pursue this finding at the end of this trial although the strategy of adding procyclidine/placebo was incorporated as a side issue in a later study (Johnstone *et al*. 1988*a*), and again an exacerbation of positive symptoms in association with procyclidine was demonstrated.

Subsequent pharmacological developments

At the time at which both studies (Johnstone *et al*. 1978*b*, 1983) were conducted, the psychopharmacology of acute schizophrenia was dominated by the idea of the relevance of D_2 receptor blockade. Indeed, the efforts of the pharmaceutical industry were directed towards synthesizing purer

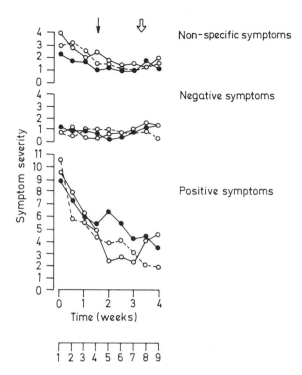

Fig. 3–3. Changes in non-specific, negative schizophrenic, and positive schizophrenic symptoms during treatment with flupenthixol and procyclidine/placebo. ↓, introduction of procyclidine/placebo. ⇩, all patients receiving placebo + standard procyclidine are on standard by this point. ●——●, active procyclidine (non-specific symptoms, $n = 15$; negative, $n = 11$; positive, $n = 16$). ○——○, placebo (non-specific symptoms $n = 11$; negative, $n = 10$; positive, $n = 12$). ○– – –○ placebo + standard (non-specific symptoms, $n = 6$; negative, $n = 5$; positive, $n = 6$).

dopamine blocking agents and eliminating other actions. As time progressed, however, it became increasingly clear that D_2 receptor blockade was not necessarily associated with improvement in clinical features. Indeed, in both of the studies referred to here there were patients with at least average levels of neuroleptic who showed substantial rises in prolactin levels but who continued to be severely psychotic. The use of and interest in atypical neuroleptics has increased following the report in 1988 of Kane *et al.* that clozapine had significantly greater benefits than chlorpromazine in treatment resistant cases. Clozapine, which has serotonin (S_2) adrenergic (α_1) histaminergic (H_1) blocking activity is a potent muscarinic acetylcholine receptor antagonist and shows relatively weak and more equivalent D_1 and D_2 receptor blocking activity as compared to standard neuroleptics (Kane *et al.* 1988). Which, if indeed any, of these known mechanisms of clozapine is relevant to its efficacy in treatment-resistant schizophrenics is not known, but this result and to some extent findings with other 'atypical neuroleptics' has stimulated interest in mechanisms of anti-psychotic effect other than D_2 receptor blockade. Against this background the demonstration of the possible serotinergic effects in the 1978 study and the cholinergic effects in the 1983 study would probably have seemed more compelling to us had they occurred now than they did when the findings were made. In spite of the dominance of the idea of dopamine receptor blockade for anti-psychotic effect, some drugs which had different mechanisms were tried for the treatment of acute positive psychotic symptoms. None of these matches standard neuroleptics in efficacy (Johnstone 1987). Carbamazepine, a potent anti-convulsant widely used in the treatment for paroxysmal pain syndromes has been reported as effective in various aspects of the management of affective illness (Post 1982). It has been suggested as a treatment for schizophrenia particularly in cases associated with violent behaviour but the evidence of its value is not strong (Donaldson *et al.* 1983). Propranolol, clonidine, and benzodiazepines were also tried in schizophrenia but again with uncertain success (Donaldson *et al.* 1983). The fact that the neuropeptide cholecystokinin has been found to coexist with dopamine in certain mesencephalic neurones assured interest in this substance as a possible treatment for schizophrenia but studies so far have not shown it to be effective (Tamminga *et al.* 1986; Montgomery and Green 1988).

Maintenance neuroleptic treatment

Neuroleptic drugs were initially used in schizophrenia for the purpose of treating the positive symptoms of acute episodes. Numerous more recent studies have focused on the role of neuroleptics in reducing schizophrenic relapse. Benefits of both oral (Leff and Wing 1971) and parenteral medication (Hirsch *et al.* 1973) have been demonstrated. In a review of 24 controlled studies Davis (1975) concluded that the evidence for efficacy of maintenance neuroleptic treatment is overwhelming. Neuroleptics, however, do not abolish susceptibility to relapse. Hogarty *et al.* (1974) followed-up patients treated with neuroleptics or placebo for two years and found a substantial effect for medication: for patients on placebo the relapse rate over two years was 80 per cent for those on neuroleptics it was 48 per cent. To exclude the possibility that this substantial relapse rate in patients on neuroleptics was due to a failure of compliance, Hogarty *et al.* (1979) conducted a later study comparing relapse rate in patients on oral neuroleptics with that in patients on depot injections whose compliance is assured. There was no difference between the two groups and the two year relapse rate remained substantial. Attempts have been made to identify factors other than neuroleptic ingestion that contribute to relapse prevention. Hogarty and colleagues (1973, 1974, 1979); Hogarty and Goldberg 1977) conducted a series of studies examining the interaction of neuroleptic therapy with social therapy designed to enhance the patients' occupational adjustment. In the 1974 study the effects of social therapy were small compared with those of neuroleptics but there was a significant tendency for those on active drugs to be less likely to relapse if they also had social therapy, and this tendency appeared to increase with time. In the 1979 study this tendency remained but was no longer significant.

Social factors and schizophrenic relapse

Brown and Birley (1968) suggested that the recurrence of schizophrenic symptoms is preceded to an unexpected degree by the occurrence of life events in the three weeks before admission. Brown *et al.* (1972) replicated these findings and demonstrated the relevance of inter-reaction between the patient and the relative with whom he lived. Relapse was more likely where 'expressed emotion' (EE) (assessed by an interview that took account of over-involvement, hostility, and critical comments on the part of the relative) was high. Vaughn and Leff (1976) extended these findings by examining EE in the key relative, time in contact with this relative, and drug therapy as they relate to relapse in the placebo-controlled trials of Leff and Wing (1971) and Hirsch *et al.* (1973). The findings suggested that patients with low EE relatives had a low liability to relapse and relatively little benefit from medication whereas patients with high EE relatives had a higher liability to relapse that was substantially reduced by active medication. In a later paper, Leff and Vaughn (1981) compared data from two studies that allowed them to consider patients developing schizophrenic episodes from high and low EE homes on and off neuroleptic medication at the time at which they became ill. Their conclusions (which they regard as speculative in view of the design and small sample size) are that susceptible individuals free from medication are liable to schizophrenic episodes in circumstances of acute stress from life events or chronic stress from living with a high EE relative. Neuroleptic drugs protect against relapse in the face of one of these stresses but not if both occur together. The findings of these studies taken together indicate that social factors may interact with neuroleptic medication to influence schizophrenic relapse. There have been a number of subsequent studies of the relationship of EE to schizophrenic relapse, some (Moline *et al.* 1985; Karno *et al.* 1987; Leff *et al.* 1987; Tarrier *et al.* 1989) supportive of the findings of Leff, Vaughn, and their co-workers and some not (Macmillan *et al.* 1986*b*; Dulz and Hand 1986; McCreadie and Robinson 1987; Parker *et al.* 1988).

The Northwick Park First Episodes Study

The interaction between EE and neuroleptic treatment in relation to relapse was one of the issues addressed by the Northwick Park Study of First Episodes of Schizophrenia (Johnstone *et al.* 1986*b*; Crow *et. al.* 1986; Macmillan *et al.* 1986*a, b*). The central element of that study was a randomized controlled trial of prophylactic neuroleptic medication following first schizophrenic episodes (Crow *et al.* 1986). Although, as mentioned above, the value of maintenance neuroleptic treatment in preventing schizophrenic relapse is well established (Davis 1975) most clinical trials of this issue indicate that a number of patients do not relapse even though they receive placebo. Nearly all such trials have included patients who have suffered more than one psychotic episode, so that it is possible that following a first schizophrenic illness, the proportion of patients who will do well without treatment is higher than the 15 to 20 per cent in those trials who remained well on placebo after one to two years. Kane *et al.* had conducted a study of the value of prophylactic neuroleptics after first schizophrenic episodes in 1982 and found an advantage at the 1 per cent level for depot fluphenazine in preventing relapse in a group of 28 patients. The beneficial effects of medication did not reach statistical significance in the 21 patients who met the Research Diagnostic Criteria of Spitzer *et al.* (1977) for schizophrenia.

The Northwick Park Study (Johnstone *et al.* 1986*b*) involved patients referred over a period of 28 months from nine medical centres. Of 462 patients referred 253 fulfilled the study criteria for first schizophrenic episodes and 120 of these entered a randomized placebo-controlled trial of maintenance neuroleptic medication on discharge; they were followed to relapse or loss to follow-up for two years, or to the end of the study. Of those on active medication 46 per cent relapsed as did 62 per cent of those on placebo ($P<0.002$). The most important determinant of relapse was duration of illness prior to starting neuroleptic medication. The time between the onset of the illness and the first trial prescription was a major determinant of relapse. Relapse was more common ($P<0.0001$) in patients where this interval was greater than one year than in those where it was less (Figs 3.4*a* and *b*)

When identified predictors of outcome were taken into account the components of EE did not significantly predict either outcome or response to medication. We interpreted this as indicating that at best such factors as EE are weak predictors of liability to relapse. This may well be so and yet this study did not provide as good a test of the value of EE as might have been expected from the sample size. More than one-third of patients lived

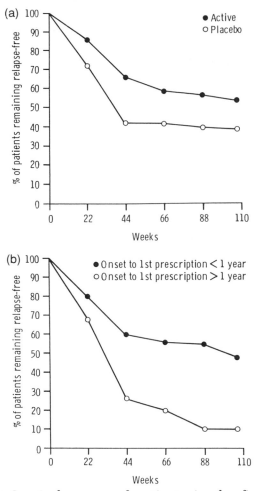

Fig. 3–4. (a) Survival curves of patients in the first episodes of schizophrenia study on active and placebo medication.
(b) Survival curves of patients in the first episodes of schizophrenia study with pre-treatment intervals of <1 year and >1 year.

alone and a further substantial proportion were of unassimilated immigrant background so that EE could only be assessed in about 30 per cent of the initial sample. Most of these young patients were unmarried and overcrowded living circumstances were uncommon. It is perhaps for these reasons that in this initially very large sample there were only six patients with high social contact and high EE, the constellation of circumstances previously found to be associated with relapse. The importance ($P<0.0001$) of the time between illness onset and the introduction of medication as a determinant of relapse was striking and somewhat unexpected, although previous findings of May *et al.* (1981) are consistent with it. In that study (May *et al.* 1981) the trial phase was confined to the period of the patients' first hospital admission, treatment subsequent to discharge being outside the investigator's control. Nevertheless, patients treated with neuroleptic drugs in the trial phase did much better in terms of outcome in the subsequent three years, but the group treated initially without drugs who spent a longer time in hospital in the trial phase did worse. In our own study, the poor outcome in patients in whom the onset-medication interval exceeded one year is particularly striking (Fig. 3.4) and those in this group maintained on active drug did not do as well as those in the short interval group maintained on placebo. There are a number of possible reasons for this. It could be that some features associated with high risk of relapse leads to delay in admission. A slow and insidious onset might lead to later admission and might be independently associated with poor outcome. Similarly, lack of social support (itself perhaps related to insidious onset) could delay hospital admission but also be related to earlier relapse after discharge. A further, more arresting possibility, is that delay in institution of treatment itself leads to a poorer long-term outcome, i.e. that persistence of symptoms untreated by neuroleptic medication leads to abnormality which cannot be completely resolved by subsequent treatment. This possibility may seem somewhat unlikely particularly as the mechanism by which such an effect could take place is entirely unclear. Nonetheless, if it were possible by early introduction of medication for the outcome in the patients with the long pre-treatment interval to be made as good is that in the patients with the short pre-treatment interval (fig. 3.4b) the benefits would be so substantial that investigation of this issue would be worth the complex trial of randomized introduction of early and late medication to patients with incipient schizophrenia that would be necessary to clarify the matter.

Although neuroleptic drugs have been of great benefit both as an acute treatment and on a maintenance basis they do have disadvantages and any development which made maintenance treatment less necessary would be beneficial. Later follow-up of the patients who entered the First Episodes of Schizophrenia Study (Johnstone *et al.* 1990) showed that in spite of significant associations between relapse and poor outcome and between relapse and placebo medication, in the patients with a relatively short pre-treatment duration of illness those on placebo medication had a significantly better outcome in occupational terms. This finding suggests the disquieting conclusion that the benefits of active neuroleptics in reducing relapse may exert a price in occupational terms. This emphasizes the need to find a more effective means of predicting which patients derive benefit from maintenance neuroleptics and which do not.

4

Questions and answers derived from the large clinical studies

The survey of schizophrenic inpatients

A number of very large clinical studies were conducted from the Division of Psychiatry, The Clinical Research Centre in Harrow, United Kingdom. The first of these was a survey of all patients of Shenley Hospital who fulfilled the St. Louis criteria (Feighner *et al.* 1972) for schizophrenia and who had been in the hospital continuously for one year or more (Owens and Johnstone 1980). Our earlier studies of small samples of patients with chronic schizophrenia had indicated that their deficits could be very severe (Frith 1977; Johnstone *et al.* 1978*a*), and we had, of course, found evidence of structural brain changes in these patients. Among the many questions raised by these early findings were those of the frequency of the severe deficits and the extent to which they are a feature of the illness itself rather than the result of other factors such as physical treatment.

It was in an attempt to answer such questions and also to provide an appropriate clinical basis for further imaging and other studies that this large survey of 510 inpatients with schizophrenia was conducted. The current condition of each patient was assessed in terms of mental state, neurological functioning, cognitive function, and behavioural performance (the assessed abnormalities). Mental state was assessed using the standardized psychiatric assessment for rating chronic psychotic patients devised by Krawiecka *et al.* (1977). This straightforward assessment was used in many of our studies. From our point of view, it is certainly reliable (Johnstone *et al.* 1987*a*) and for studies like this one has the great virtue of being able to be completed in most patients even where co-operation is very limited. An important consideration in the choice of cognitive tests was the need for most patients to achieve at least some score and our previous experience with the Withers and Hinton (1971) test battery suggested that it would be a suitable choice. Neurological functioning was assessed using the 'Scheme for Brief Neurological Assessment' which was based on the method of neurological assessment devised by Renfrew (1967) but which omitted sensory testing. Our assessment of 'behavioural performance' was intended to take account of the fact that the other assessments we conducted, being carried out on single occasions by clinicians who were often strangers to the patients, might not reflect an entirely accurate picture of the patient's overall state. The 'Current Behavioural Schedule' was therefore devised (Johnstone *et al*. 1985). It was designed to record, in a standardized way, information given by the nursing staff, about the patient's behaviour over the previous six months. There are, of course, many rating scales for long-stay patients (Hall 1980) but none of these was entirely suitable for our purpose as we wished to record the opinion of these constantly with the patients about the presence of various psychopathological features in addition to their description of the patient's behaviour. For these reasons our own rating was devised, although it was partly based upon the behaviour rating scale of Wing (1961).

After the 'assessed abnormalities' had been completed detailed historical information was recorded from the casenotes. The features of the illness at its worst were recorded by the application of the 'Syndrome Check List of the Present State Examination' (Wing *et al*. 1974) to the relevant part of the notes. Demographic details were noted and a number of items of personal and family history and details of past treatment were recorded in a standardized manner. Some of this information was obtained from an 'enquiry form' which relatives had been required to complete at the time of admission and which frequently provided detailed information. Details of psychosurgery, insulin coma treatment, and electroconvulsive therapy (ECT) had been carefully recorded in the casenotes, and drug cards dating back to the 1930s were available.

Considerable morbidity in terms of mental state abnormalities was demonstrated, only 32 patients showing no rating within the morbid range on the Krawiecka *et al*. (1977) scale. Similarly severe impairments were found on cognitive testing, the patients performing substantially less well than control samples. More than 70 per cent of patients showed some neurological abnormality, in most cases a disorder of movement or tone. Major impairments of behavioural performance were described by the nursing staff although, as in all of the assessments, the range of abnormality was wide (Owens and Johnstone 1980). The items of historical information used in calculating relationships between past events and current abnormalities are shown in Table 4.1.

Insulin and ECT were recorded as 'none', 'some', or 'much'; some being less than the mean number of treatments for the group and much being more. The mean number of treatments for insulin coma was 61, the range being from 1 to 206. The mean number of treatments for ECT was 23, the range being from 1 to 234. The 234 treatments were given to one man in a continuous course. Psychosurgery was largely confined to leucotomy, although one patient had leucotomy and transection of the fornix and another had two leucotomies. For the purposes of the calculation leucotomy was recorded as performed or not. Neuroleptic treatment was recorded as 'none', 'some', or 'much' in terms of specified dose ranges

(Owens and Johnstone 1980). The assessed abnormalities were related to one another and to the items of recorded information. There were no significant relationships between positive features of schizophrenia (delusions, hallucinations, incongruity of affect, and incoherence of speech, as rated on the Krawiecka *et al.* 1977 scale, but there were highly significant relationships between all of the other assessed abnormalities, see Fig. 4.1.

Mental state features related to the features of the illness at its worst so that positive features at interview were worse in those whose initial illnesses were categorized as NS or DS (nuclear or definite) rather than CS (catatonic) (Wing *et al.* 1974) and negative features were worse in those with initial catatonic illnesses. There was a significant positive correlation between negative features and duration of illness ($P<0.01$). Cognitive functioning related to the features of illness at its worst, being most poor in those with initial catatonic illnesses. The only other significant relationships

Table 4–1 *Recorded information used in the survey of 510 Shenley inpatient schizophrenics*

Historical variables	Treatment variables
Age (mean, 59.2 + 13.9 yrs)	Insulin coma (none, 310; some, 81; much, 57)
Age at onset (mean, 28.2 + 8.9 yrs)	
Duration of illness *(mean, 31 + 11.1 yrs)*	*ECT* *(none, 281; some, 119; much, 41)*
Duration of current hospitalization (mean, 26.5 + 13.1 yrs)	
Family history of schizophrenia (none, 217; probable, 67; definite, 65)	Neuroleptics (none, 65; some, 140; much, 305)
Birth trauma/head injury (stated, 70; not stated, 231)	Leucotomy (performed, 42; none, 425)
Fits (yes, 56; no, 323)	
Past academic record (university or equiv., 31; average, 314; poor, 46)	
Course of illness (worse, 76; no change, 298; beter, 42)	
PSE* categorization (almost all, NS; DS; DP, or CS)	

* PSE, Present State Examination.

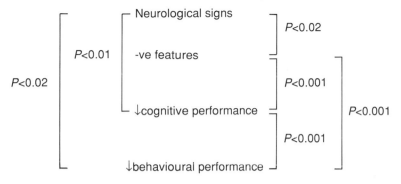

+ve features - NS

Fig. 4–1. Relationships between assessed abnormalities in the Survey of Schizophrenic Inpatients (Owens and Johnstone 1980).

between cognitive functioning and items of recorded information concerned age (negative correlation, $P<0.01$), duration of illness (negative correlation, $P<0.001$) insulin treatment (much insulin $>$ no insulin, $P<0.05$), and past academic record (university or equivalent $>$ average, $P<0.001$; university or equivalent $>$ poor, $P<0.001$; average $>$ poor, $P<0.001$). The finding concerning insulin coma treatment is unexpected as clearly it might be anticipated that the hypoglycaemia associated with this treatment could result in brain damage and cognitive impairment (Marks and Rose 1965). Examination of the casenotes revealed that insulin coma tended to be reserved for patients with good pre-morbid function (indeed it seemed to be particularly often used for university students), and it appeared likely that selection criteria for the treatment accounted for this result. Neurological variables were considered separately for those on and off neuroleptics and anti-cholinergics at the time of examination and the significant relationships with recorded information essentially concerned age and duration of illness. The only significant relationships between behavioural performance and recorded information concerned the features of the illness at its worst with performance being most poor in those with initial catatonic illnesses.

In general, therefore, these patients were very much impaired by wide-ranging disabilities. Although there was no reason to believe that they were atypical, in terms of their socioeconomic background or education, of the general population of chronically hospitalized patients in the United Kingdom at that time, the fact that some of them had not been exposed to neuroleptics or other physical treatments by the late 1970s was certainly unusual. Otherwise, the treatment regimes that had been employed were probably not atypical. The fact that none of the assessed abnormalities significantly related to past physical treatments was a surprise to the investigators. We had anticipated that the profound impairments of behaviour and intellectual functioning would be shown in part to be associated with extensive physical treatment. It has been established that severe behavioural and intellectual deficits can result from profound or prolonged hypoglycaemia (Marks and Rose 1965) and marked behaviour disorganization was a significant complication of leucotomy, especially in the earlier procedures (May 1974). It has been suggested that large numbers of ECTs can result in permanent cognitive deficits (Friedberg 1977). The role of neuroleptics in producing movement disorders has, of course, been widely discussed (Crane and Paulson 1966; FDA Task Force 1973) and furthermore it was suggested that neuroleptics may cause more widespread damage to the nervous system (Marsden 1976). In spite of all of these findings the only items of recorded information which had any bearing on assessed abnormalities in our study were the features of the illness at its worst, past academic record, and factors relating to time. It appeared that past physical treatment had not produced the current deficits. It was concluded that these deficits are either an integral part of the disease process or the result of other external factors which have been in operation since the patient first became ill—or possibly a combination of the two.

The effects of long-stay care

It has long been recognized (Kety 1959) that hospital care may be associated with factors, such as dietary anomalies, chronic infection, and altered activity, which may cause changes that can erroneously be attributed to the basic disease process. In patients with chronic schizophrenia there is the further difficulty that the typical features of the disorder include shallowness of emotional response and lack of motivation which are difficult to distinguish from aspects of behaviour and attitudes said to result from long-term institutional care (Wing and Brown 1970). The possibility that institutional care may interact with the deficits of schizophrenia and intensify the social withdrawal and lack of motivation of patients with this disorder was discussed by Myerson (1939) and later by Martin (1955) and Barton (1959). The latter used the term 'institutional neurosis' to describe the morbid features which may be found in patients who have been in mental hospitals or other restricted environments. He listed these features as apathy, social withdrawal, deterioration of personal habits, and postural abnormalities. While he suggested that these abnormalities may develop in anyone who lives for prolonged periods in such environments, the patients in whom he actually observed these features suffered from schizophrenia and were indeed Shenley patients, the same hospital as that used for our survey (Owens and Johnstone 1980). The difficulty of separating the contribution of the schizophrenic process from that of its institutional care was apparent to Barton, but the abnormalities which have been said to be the typical results of living in an institution are clearly similar to at least some of those found in our survey of schizophrenic inpatients.

In an attempt to resolve the matter of whether the abnormalities are an integral part of the schizophrenic process or result from some external factor perhaps relating to the circumstances of care, two additional groups of patients were examined in exactly the same way as the inpatients with chronic schizophrenia. Those groups were: (1) patients with schizophrenia who had not received long-term inpatient care; and (2) patients who had received long-term inpatient care in Shenley Hospital but who did not have schizophrenia. The first group was derived by examining the records of all patients discharged from Shenley between 1970 and 1975 and selecting those who fulfilled the St. Louis criteria (Feighner *et al.* 1972) for schizophrenia (Johnstone *et al.* 1981). There were 120 such patients. Many were found to have had further episodes of inpatient care since their discharge in 1970–74, but none had been continuously hospitalized for as long as one year since that time and thus there was no overlap in this respect between this sample and those in the inpatient survey. Historical details were recorded from the casenotes exactly as for the inpatient sample. Of the patients, 105 were successfully traced and those who were alive, living in the United Kingdom, and consented were examined in exactly the same way as the inpatients, usually in their own homes, the behavioural schedule being completed on the basis of an interview with a relative rather than a nurse. A quantity of additional social information was obtained in those discharged patients.

The second additional group of patients were identified at the same time as those in the inpatient schizophrenic sample. Of the 1227 inpatients in Shenley Hospital at that time 29 fulfilled the St. Louis criteria (Feighner *et al.* 1972) for primary affective illness, had been inpatients continuously for at least one year and remained in hospital for long enough to be examined. The historical information and examination variables were recorded exactly as in the other two groups. The three groups of patients differed in terms of age and duration of illness and correction was made for these differences. When this was done there were no differences between the two groups of schizophrenics in terms of positive or negative features or the individual items of the current behavioural schedule, but the inpatients performed significantly less well on cognitive tests (Johnstone *et al.* 1981, 1985). On the other hand, the manic-depressive inpatients had significantly less severe positive and negative features than the schizophrenic inpatients and showed a significantly different pattern of behaviour on the individual items of the current behavioural schedule but both groups were equally cognitively impaired (Johnstone *et al.* 1985). These results were interpreted as indicating that in patients who suffer schizophrenic illnesses which conform to the St. Louis Criteria (Feighner *et al.* 1972), positive and negative symptoms may well be continuing features whether or not long-term institutional care takes place. Institutional care may be associated with worse cognitive deficits but there was no evidence that it increased the other abnormalities. It was concluded that, apart from those involving cognition, the severe deficits found in the survey of schizophrenic inpatients were due to the disease process from which these patients suffered and not to the circumstances of its treatment. It is of interest that these results find support in the recent study of Curson *et al*, (1992) in which no relationship was found between poverty of the social environment in an institution and 'clinical poverty', i.e. negative schizophrenic features, such as blunted affect, poverty of speech and social withdrawal.

Social consequences of schizophrenia

As noted above, substantial additional social information was obtained on the discharged schizophrenic patients (Johnstone *et al*. 1984). They were often interviewed at home and their relatives were seen at some length. The difficulties of schizophrenic patients discharged to the community and the problems experienced by their relatives' had been quite widely described by the time this study was conducted in 1979–80 (Creer and Wing 1974; Creer 1975; Cheadle *et al*. 1978; NSF 1979) and the investigators were experienced in interviewing schizophrenic patients and their relatives. In spite of this I think all of us involved in the home visits found this a disturbing study to conduct and I think that the details of some of these interviews will be etched in my mind for ever. The tragic decline of the patients in the inpatient study was of course evident but when patients are seen in large numbers in a hospital setting the contrast between their current state and what it might have been without the illness is not nearly so obvious as when the patient is seen in his home circumstances against the background of his well relatives. Ordinary clinical interviews with relatives are often intended to be supportive, to emphasize any positive aspects of the situation and to encourage the relatives to carry on helping the patient with managing outside the hospital. The relatives are generally not encouraged to describe with examples just how limited or difficult to live with the patient really is. In these interviews they were encouraged to do just that and what they had to say did not make easy listening for those involved in the mental health services. While there were many dramatic (although I do not think at all exaggerated) tales of disorganized, destructive, and frightening behaviour, I was more saddened by the matter-of-fact accounts of just what it is like to live with a very limited, affectively flattened, and withdrawn relative. A number of the patients were housewives and were described by their husbands as coping reasonably. When additional details were requested, these men explained that their wives prepared meals from a range of only four or five dishes, could not shop unaided, and never offered any spontaneous conversation. I well remember a policeman in his thirties who described his wife (the mother of his sons aged 11 and 8 years) as managing not too badly, laughing wryly when I asked him how his wife would react if he asked her to make him a coffee or cup of tea while he was watching TV in the evening. He explained to me, clearly surprised by my lack of understanding, that such a request would put his wife into a state of indecision and uncertainty that would last for days and went on to explain to me in response to another probably inept question that he could not remember when his wife had last greeted him when he went home or when she had last shown any spontaneous interest in his work or other activities. This lack of ability to show interest in relatives' activity or well-being was very widely described once enquired for, but informants did not volunteer it, as it was very apparent from many aspects of the interview that the relatives' expectations of the patients' behaviour had become sadly low. Many of them felt that the services had been less than helpful and, while some of the problems may well have resulted from issues, such as the difficulty of the relatives in coming to terms with the prognosis of the illness, some of their more bitter remarks did have the ring of truth. We were repeatedly told that the services were keen to be involved with the patients when they first became ill, but that they lost interest when time passed and the patients did not become well. The relatives did not think that those concerned realized how great a burden was being placed on families when patients were discharged. One man spoke for many when he said: 'You people don't know what you're doing when you let these folks out, looking after them is a full-time job—a full-time job done by amateurs with damn all help from anyone'.

At a less anecdotal level, this study (Johnstone *et al.* 1984) showed some interesting findings. The results showed that recovery from schizophrenia can take place even in patients fulfilling the St. Louis criteria (Feighner *et al.* 1972) which include at least six months of reduced function as an obligatory feature. At follow-up, 18 per cent of the sample had normal mental states and evidently functioned entirely normally. Almost all of those well patients were female, a finding which is consistent with the report of Watt *et al.* (1983). This degree of well-being is less than that reported by Leff and Vaughn (1972), but is a good deal higher than the 3 per cent reported by McCreadie (1982). Nonetheless, between five and nine years following discharge over 50 per cent of this sample (from which the currently re-admitted had been eliminated) remained clearly psychotic and by all available accounts many were consistently and severely impaired.

In spite of their disabilities and difficulties the patients did not want to go back to hospital and indeed the relatives rarely wished them to return there. In view of the great difficulties that the relatives often described, this lack of enthusiasm for hospital care does not speak well of their previous experiences of hospital management. Further causes of concern raised by this part of the study were the number of psychotic patients in social difficulty who were not in touch with any service, the apparent uneven allocation of care, and the number of unmet needs, particularly of relatives.

Clinical and social aspects of the first episodes study

The studies described so far in this chapter concerned patients who had been ill for some years, sometimes for decades, when the investigators first met them. We were much impressed by their impairments and by the contrast between their level of function when they were examined and the level that they might have been expected to have on the basis of their history, or on the basis of the functioning of their relatives. Our next study concerned patients referred with what were thought to be first schizophrenic episodes. They were seen at the time of their first episodes between 1979 and 1981 (Johnstone *et al*. 1986*b*) for follow-up two years later (Macmillan *et al*. 1986*a*; Johnstone *et al*. 1990), and a number were involved in the large follow-up study conducted between 1988 and 1990 and were thus seen for the 10 year follow-up. The investigators therefore had the opportunity to study the progress of these illnesses from the beginning and to compare their later condition with the way they were on recovering from the first episode when they and their relatives often thought that they were 'back to normal'. The view is sometimes expressed (Murray and Lewis 1987) that schizophrenic patients with a defect state have always been impaired and that their limitations reflect pre-illness evidence of developmental abnormality rather than sequelae of illness. Having seen markedly deteriorated social habits, apathy, and blunted and empty affective responses develop in patients I have known, such as an elegant and polished air hostess, two charming if shy ex-public schoolboys, one studying law and the other accountancy, and a bright-eyed engineering apprentice with a fondness for flashy clothes, I know that this idea is at least sometimes quite wrong. Aside from the interest in drug-related and family factors on relapse the main information derived from the first episodes study concerned the nature of the episodes and those that they affected, the outcome of the generality of cases, and the effectiveness or otherwise of the health services in the management of illnesses of this kind. Patients were referred over 28 months from nine collaborating medical centres within a 20 mile radius of the Clinical Research Centre, Northwick Park. Clinicians were asked to refer any patient aged between 15 and 70 years with a first psychotic illness, not unequivocally affective and not obviously organic. Many assessments were conducted (Johnstone *et al*. 1986*b*) including the Present State Examination (PSE) (Wing *et al*. 1974) and only patients fulfilling criteria for schizophrenic or paranoid categories on PSE/CATEGO were included. Other inclusion criteria were admission for at least one week, no past history of psychosis or possible psychosis of any kind, and the absence of organic disease with definite or possible aetiological significance.

Altogether, 462 patients were referred. Somewhat surprisingly, 65 of them were found to have had an initially undeclared previous psychotic episode, 64 could not, for various reasons, co-operate with the PSE, the diagnosis was not confirmed in 62 cases, and in 15 patients an organic condition, of definite or possible aetiological significance and not initially suspected, was found to be present. The occurrence of apparently typical schizophrenic illnesses which are associated and may be due to established organic disease has received substantial interest (Davison and Bagley 1969; Davison 1983). This interest is not because such illnesses are thought to be common (what evidence there is would be consistent with the figures of 6 per cent found in this study) but because of the possibility that the mechanism underlying these illnesses where clear pathology can be demonstrated might shed light on the pathogenesis of the generality of schizophrenia. Certainly, some at least of those 15 cases demonstrated psychopathology which would have been considered entirely typical of schizophrenia, and had it not been for the demonstration of organic illness they would have fulfilled operational criteria for schizophrenia, but the illnesses were diverse and it was difficult to envisage a final common pathway by which they could have given rise to an often very similar pattern of psychopathology.

Among the many items of information sought from the relatives was the nature and timing of the onset. The interval between onset and admission varied considerably and in many cases was surprisingly long. One of the most distressing aspects of this study was the relatives' account of just how very difficult a period this interval was. To try to quantify this difficulty, assessments of social withdrawal and disturbed behaviour and a count of the number of contacts with helping services before that which led directly to hospital admission were made. Social withdrawal was profound in 43 patients and actively disturbed behaviour was common (Johnstone *et al.* 1986*b*) behaviour potentially threatening to life of the patient occurring in 64 cases and behaviour potentially threatening to the lives of others in 48 cases. The behaviour that these figures represent was not trivial; that threatening to the patient's life includes attempted hanging, actual or attempted self-poisoning, lying on the centre lane of a motorway, etc. Behaviour threatening to the lives of others ranged from an ill-organized attempt to hurl an iron bar at a neighbour because of delusions of misidentification, to a prolonged attack occurring over the course of hours where a patient inflicted multiple wounds with a knife and a walking stick upon his father in the belief that he was the Devil; the father, who had required blood transfusion, discharged himself from hospital against medical advice, to arrange for the patient's admission which had not yet taken place.

Admission was effected for 73 patients after zero, one, or two prior contacts but in 46 cases, at least nine prior contacts were made with at least one service before admission was arranged. The maximum number of contacts was 33, these being made on behalf of her son by a sensible, articulate and, by the time I met her, angry and bitter Irish lady. The son had locked himself in his room almost all of the time for months and refused to communicate in any way with anyone who called. When finally admitted to hospital he was filthy and weighed six stones (38 kg). The mother had kept copies of the letters she had written to various doctors, social services agencies, the Department of Health, her Member of Parliament, and others together with their replies. She agreed to my copying these documents. The reply which she had found most helpful and which was really the only one to contain practical advice was from the editor of the problem page of a women's magazine.

The short-term outcome in these patients was worse than we had expected. We had had some uncertainties about the design of the study wondering if our criteria were not sufficiently stringent. We had thought that the sample might include numbers of patients with what would turn out to be very brief psychotic episodes which would do well and would not in retrospect fulfil operational criteria for schizophrenia. Such a finding would have made it difficult to interpret the results of the drug trial. The findings were in fact very different. Seventeen patients did not achieve discharge within the two year study period and thus could not be considered for the trial and a further 34 required inpatient care for over six months. Sixty per cent relapsed within two years, and at follow up 50 per cent were employed in some capacity. At the onset, there were 85 children under the age of 16 who were the offspring of the patients assessed. At follow-up only 50 per cent of those children lived in a nuclear family setting. Four patients died during follow-up, none from natural causes, and judicial charges of murder, actual bodily harm, malicious damage, indecent exposure, theft, and illegal immigration were brought in the case of seven discharged patients and a Section 60 was requested for one other patient (Macmillan *et al*. 1986*a*). It did seem, therefore, that even at this early stage of schizophrenia the outcome for many patients assessed in various ways was poor but it was not poor in every case. The median age of this sample was 25 years, a time of life at which educational, occupational, and social achievement might be expected; some assessment of this was made. Ten cases made definite attainments, two completed further educational courses, one completed 'O' Levels at night school, three achieved promotion at work (a musician, a lecturer, and in the motor manufacturing industry), two entered stable relationships, and one achieved work compatible with his high pre-morbid intelligence, and resumed his doctoral theses. Three cases achieved less, one limited youth started an industrial rehabilitation course, one man who had never previously lived alone maintained his former occupation as a dustman and lived in his own flat, and a third man (previously a university undergraduate) obtained a place at a polytechnic. Thirteen patients thus made definite or possible achievements but in the remainder there is no record of activity which could be claimed as achievement even in these modest terms. A more systematic study of outcome in those 253 patients concerned number of days spent as an inpatient over the next two years, and occupation at follow-up relative to their best occupational level, in terms of the Registrar General's classification (Johnstone *et al.* 1990). Poor outcome in these terms was in general associated with social withdrawal, inactivity, and poor social presentation at onset, and with more soft neurological signs at that time. The other principal finding of this aspect of the study was the significant association in patients with a relatively short pre-treatment duration of illness between better outcome in occupational terms, and placebo rather than active medication in spite of the significant associations between relapse and poor outcome and relapse and placebo medication. This was a new finding because placebo-controlled follow-up studies of first episodes of schizophrenia are uncommon. It suggested the disquieting conclusion that the benefits of active neuroleptics in reducing relapse may exact a price in occupational terms.

Questions arising from these studies

These large studies answer some questions but raise others. Schizophrenia is thought of as being a mental illness characterized by certain psychotic features at the onset, normally, until now at least, without a demonstrable underlying anatomical or physiological cause, and with a variable course leading, usually, to a poor outcome. These studies certainly showed that such disorders remain common and they showed that the various operational criteria for schizophrenia do indeed, in general, predict a poor outcome. Just a few patients, however, appear to achieve sustained recovery and we do not yet know how to predict those whose illness will take this course. The importance of this is emphasized by the findings showing the occupational cost of maintenance neuroleptics. The nature of the psychopathological features associated with loss of independence, unemployment, and impairment requires further definition. Cognitive impairments were associated with the features of the defect state but did occur in patients with manic-depressive illness as well as those with schizophrenia and were less marked in patients living outside of hospital. We do not know whether the circumstances of life as an inpatient emphasize cognitive decline, or whether patients who develop cognitive impairments in association with a psychotic illness of whatever kind will be so incapacitated that they will require continued care from others. It is evident from the earlier studies that cognitive decline is a feature of the schizophrenic defect state but how central it is to that condition is unclear. The unsuspected organic conditions in the first episodes study did not offer any clues to the aetiology of schizophrenia but are tantalizing nevertheless. The possibility that more cases have such illnesses seems unlikely but is difficult to exclude entirely and, of course, imaging and other neuropathological studies suggest that there is an organic basis to many cases even although we cannot always detect it with present techniques.

5

The 'Functional' Psychosis Studies: what are the boundaries of schizophrenia?

It is clear from the work described in the previous chapter that it is far from easy to find defining characteristics for the concept of schizophrenia. The clinical and social outcome is poor, in many respects, in the majority of cases, but some patients, even among those who have at one time shown chronic deterioration of function for at least six months, do appear to recover (Johnstone *et al.* 1981). Cognitive impairments are marked in some schizophrenic patients, but not all, and appear to be a feature of chronically institutionalized manic depressive patients as well as of schizophrenic patients receiving similar care (Johnstone *et al.* 1985). Many acute schizophrenic episodes respond to dopamine blocking agents but some show little or no response (Macmillan *et al.* 1986*a*) and while maintenance neuroleptics are of value to many schizophrenic patients, relapse is common, even in those where compliance is assured. Moreover, some patients remain well without medication of this kind. An organic illness of definite or possible aetiological significance is found in a small percentage of schizophrenic patients. Although it is possible that there are more cases in whom such processes exist but are undetected it is unlikely that this widespread.

The series of investigations described as the Northwick Park 'Functional' Psychosis Studies was designed to try to examine the boundaries of schizophrenia, particularly in relation to manic-depressive psychosis. The main criterion which Kraepelin used to separate dementia praecox from the various forms of manic-depressive insanity was poor prognosis but he did find that a small minority of his dementia praecox patients did not deteriorate in this way and that a good outcome was occasionally possible. Both Kasanin (1933) and E. Bleuler (1911/1950) recognized that a substantial proportion of functionally psychotic patients fitted neatly into neither the category of schizophrenia nor that of manic-depressive psychosis, having features suggestive of both disorders. The term schizoaffective psychosis was introduced to describe such cases by Kasanin in 1933 and it has been widely used since, but it is rarely clearly defined and the level of agreement across various definitions of this and related terms is low (Brockington and

Leff 1979). At present, the only criteria which can be used to validate the diagnoses of schizophrenia and manic-depressive psychosis are outcome and response to drug treatment. These criteria have been used in attempts to decide whether schizoaffective disorder is a form of schizophrenia or a form of affective disorder (Welner *et al.* 1974; Procci 1976; Pope and Lipinski 1978). To use treatment response to support such diagnostic decisions and to derive theories concerning neurochemical dysfunction as a basis for functional psychosis would be an appropriate strategy if there were evidence indicating that schizophrenia, mania, and psychotic depression respond differently to drug treatments. Such evidence is lacking. It is established that neuroleptic drugs are an effective treatment for acute schizophrenia (NIMH 1964) and that lithium is an effective treatment for mania (Stokes *et al.* 1971) and perhaps also for depression (Mendels 1975). Neuroleptics are of established efficacy in the treatment of mania (Prien *et al.* 1972*a*) and patients who are depressed and deluded may respond at least as well to neuroleptics as to tricyclic anti-depressants (Brockington *et al.* 1978, 1980). It has been argued that the effects of lithium are specific to the affective disorders (Schou 1963) but studies have suggested that lithium may be of value in schizophrenia (Alexander *et al.* 1979; Hirschowitz *et al.* 1980) and schizo-affective disorders (Prien *et al.* 1972*b*) and it has also been reported that a combination of lithium and neuroleptics is better than neuroleptic alone in the treatment of schizophrenia (Small *et al.* 1975; Biederman *et al.* 1979). Interpretation of the studies of lithium in schizophrenia and schizoaffective states has been limited by small sample sizes, the scarcity of adequate controlled trials, and the lack of agreement about the diagnosis of schizoaffective disorder (Prien 1979; Delva and Letemendia 1982).

The 'Functional' Psychosis Studies

These studies were designed to clarify the relationships between categorization within the broad class of functional psychosis, response to drug treatment and outcome in the short and medium term.

Patients were selected from all of those admitted under the care of the participating clinicians with definite or possible psychosis over a four year period (Johnstone *et al.* 1988*a*). No diagnostic categorizations were applied. Standardized documentation and assessment was carried out on all patients admitted until 120 of them had been entered in the drug trial which was the first investigation (Johnstone *et al.* 1988*a*). These 120 patients were selected from 360 admissions of 326 individuals (see Fig. 5.1). Each of the 120 patients was assessed before and throughout the study for psychotic symptoms, manic symptoms, and depressive symptoms. Before randomization, the sample was subdivided into patients with predominantly elevated

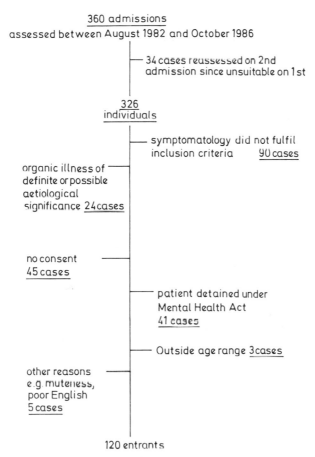

Fig. 5–1. Derivation of cases in Functional Psychosis Study (Johnstone *et al.* 1988*a*).

mood, predominantly depressed mood, and those with no consistent mood change. Within this substratification the patients were randomly and blindly allocated to: (a) pimozide plus lithium; (b) placebo pimozide plus lithium; (c) pimozide plus placebo lithium; and (d) placebo pimozide plus placebo lithium. Pimozide was the chosen neuroleptic because it is a relatively pure dopamine blocking agent. Treatment was continued for four weeks. There was a highly significant effect of pimozide upon positive psychotic symptoms ($P<0.00001$) and this occurred whatever the mood state of the patient (Fig. 5.2). Pimozide had no significant effect upon negative symptoms elevation of mood or depression of mood. Conversely, lithium had no significant effect upon positive symptoms either in the group as a whole or in the individual mood categories separately and had no effects upon negative or depressive symptoms. It did, however, have a significant effect in reducing elevation of mood (*P*<0.02). It appeared, therefore, that in this study the effects of pimozide were upon a group of symptoms and were not diagnosis-specific. There was no evidence that response to neuroleptics was a defining characteristic of the diagnosis of schizophrenia.

The situation as far as lithium is concerned was less straightforward. The Bech–Rafaelsen *et al.* (1978) scale (on which elevation of mood was assessed) identifies a group of symptoms which points to a diagnosis of mania but some score on this scale is achieved by patients who would not be diagnosed as manic by any system. It is only when those patients were included that the result concerning the efficacy of lithium became significant. It cannot be said, therefore, that the effects of lithium were diagnosis-specific while those of pimozide were not, but the effects of lithium were rather more clearly related to diagnosis than those of the dopamine blocker. Reclassification of the patients sample using PSE/CATEGO (Wing *et al.* 1974) and DSM III (APA 1980) did not affect the findings. The study was conducted in order to examine the value of treatment response as a validating criterion for diagnosis. The significant effect of pimozide in treating positive symptoms in patients in whom elevated mood and depressed mood are predominant as well as in those with no mood change. The similarity of this effect in these three groups and the fact that these findings were not changed if the patients were classified in terms of PSE/CATEGO or DSM III instead of the simple study subclassification, supported the idea that positive symptoms, in the setting of functional psychosis, are relieved by dopaminergic blockade regardless of the form of the psychosis. Taken in

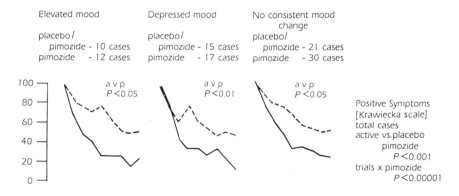

Fig. 5–2. Improvement in positive symptoms with pimozide in patients with elevated mood, depressed mood, and with no consistent mood change.

isolation the effects of pimozide in this study could be held to support the alternative view to the binary position of Kraepelin, namely that functional psychosis is a continuum (Crow 1986). This concept is supported by the failure of Kendell and colleagues (1970, 1980) to achieve a bimodal separation of schizophrenia and affective psychosis on the basis of symptoms or outcome. The study also concerned the effects of lithium and the results as a whole suggest that at least two processes are involved in these disorders, one concerned with dopaminergic mechanisms and positive symptoms and the other not demonstrably associated with positive symptoms but concerned with the stabilization of elevated mood and related to a mechanism which lithium has and pimozide has not.

The maintenance phase

This drug trial was continued into a maintenance phase which concerned those patients who participated in the acute phase of the 'Functional' Psychosis Study, completed their four week period of acute treatment, achieved an arbitrary standard of recovery and were prepared to continue on a trial regimen for some considerable time (until two years after the last patient had entered phase 1—an interval which amounted to six years in the first case). These criteria reduced the sample size considerably and the investigation concerned a total of 30 patients (Johnstone *et al*. 1991*a*). This meant that it was not really appropriate to consider the results of the maintenance phase in terms of diagnostic subdivisions and we were not able to consider whether or not response to maintenance treatment, with lithium, pimozide, both active preparations or placebo could be used as a validation of diagnosis of schizophrenia or manic-depressive psychosis. The principal question addressed by the study, therefore, was the relative value for prophylaxis against relapse of lithium, pimozide, and placebo in a population of patients with functional psychosis who had achieved a satisfactory response in the acute phase to the medication they later received on a maintenance basis. Pimozide was significantly more effective than placebo pimozide in preventing relapse (*P*=0.01). No significant effect of lithium was found but this may reflect the fact that relatively few of the patients had illnesses which would have fulfilled criteria for affective illness (Johnstone *et al*. 1991*a*). It was evident that prophylactic neuroleptic medication was of value even in patients who had recovered from an acute episode of psychosis without active neuroleptic and that an acute response of this kind did not identify a group of patients who could be predicted to remain well without active medication.

Organic aspects

As noted in Chapter 4 the nature of the organic disorder in the patients referred for the Northwick Park First Episodes Study (Johnstone *et al.* 1986*b*) was examined in detail (Johnstone *et al.* 1987*b*) partly in the hope that light might thus be shed upon the pathogenesis of the generality of schizophrenia. The cases were diverse, however, and it was difficult to envisage a final common path by which they could have given rise to an often very similar pattern of psychopathology. Twenty-three of the patients considered for the Functional Psychosis Study were found to have organic illness of at least possible aetiological significance and spoke adequate English. Comparison was made between the phenomenology of these organic cases and 92 matched controls drawn from the parent samples who conformed to DSM III criteria for schizophrenia, mania, and depression (Johnstone *et al.* 1988*b*). Few significant differences were present and there was considerable overlap between the diagnostic groups. This result is of limited relevance to the principal issue addressed by 'Functional' Psychosis Studies, namely the exploration of validating criteria for the diagnostic subdivision of functional psychoses. The fact that the causes underlying the 23 organic cases in functional psychosis sample showed considerable similarities with the 15 cases from the first episode sample (see Table 5.1) suggests that classification of the pathogenesis of these organically based cases is unlikely to be helpful in clarifying the boundaries of schizophrenia and affective psychoses. While the phenemonology of the first episode cases in Table 5.1 was often very typical of schizophrenia (Johnstone *et al.* 1987*b*) some of the 23 cases from the 'functional' psychosis sample with the same underlying disorders presented a picture which could have been considered typical of mania or psychotic depression as well as of schizophrenia.

Outcome as a validating criterion of diagnosis

The main aim of the 'Functional' Psychosis Studies was to investigate the value of both treatment response and outcome as validating criteria for the diagnoses of schizophrenia and manic-depressive psychosis. Treatment response could, of course, only be assessed in the cases who entered the drug trial but more patients could be included when the issue of outcome was considered. In this part of the investigation we addressed the relationship between classification within the broad category of functional psychosis and outcome two and a half years later. Outcome was examined in social, clinical, and cognitive terms. We considered whether outcome in these terms may appropriately be used as a validation of the specific diagnostic categories of schizophrenia, affective disorder, and schizoaffective

Table 5–1 Nature of organic diagnosis in Northwick Park studies of first schizophrenic episodes or of 'Functional' Psychoses

Diagnosis	1st episodes of schizophrenia: 15 cases (Johnstone et al. 1987)	'Functional' psychoses: 23 cases (Johnstone et al. 1988b)
Alcohol excess	3	2
Drug abuse/Withdrawal	2	10
Syphilis	3	1
Carcinoma of the lung	1	1
Autoimune multisystem disease (SLE)	1	1
Thyrotoxicosis	1	1
Cerebrovascular accident	1	1
Sarcoidosis	2	
Epilepsy/Cerebral cysticercosis	1	
Hypothyroidism		1
Intracranial tumour		2
Ulcerative colitis on steroids		1
Vitamin B^{12} deficiency		1
Uncontrolled diabetes mellitus		1

psychosis as derived by the later application of two separate diagnostic systems to the information concerning the index admission. Lastly, the relationships between clinical and cognitive assessments at the time of the 2.5 year follow-up were examined. Of the original 326 patients assessed for the 'Functional' Psychosis Study at the time patients were being recruited for the drug trial (Johnstone *et al.* 1988a) 260 could be traced 2.5 years later (Johnstone *et al.* 1992). Diagnostic criteria were applied at the close of the study (Johnstone *et al.* 1992) and those patients with index diagnostic classifications which could be considered to fall under the broad headings of schizophrenia, mania, depressive illness, and schizoaffective disorder were included when the relationship between outcome and categorization was examined. The design whereby the diagnostic classifications were derived after the follow-up had been completed was intended to reduce the likelihood of preconceptions about the outcome of differing diagnostic categories from influencing the situation. Patients whose index classification was in a schizophrenic category had higher doses of neuroleptics, prescribed for longer periods than other patients, had longer durations of inpatient and day patient care, and during the follow-up period worked for shorter periods than those in other groups. The occupational functioning of the schizophrenic patients during the follow-up period was significantly worse than those in the other groups. More unexpected was the finding that at their best the schizophrenic patients worked in capacities as skilled as those of the patients with affective illness (see Fig. 5.3).

In terms of the mental state assessments conducted at the 2.5 year follow-up both positive and negative symptoms were worse in schizophrenic groups. There were no differences between the diagnostic groups in terms of the Bech–Rafaelsen (1978) score for elevated mood but patients whose index episode was classed as schizophrenic or depressed had significantly higher scores than the other groups on the Montgomery–Asberg (1979) score for depression. A wide range of psychological tests involving nine separate assessments was conducted but the only significant difference between the diagnostic groups was that schizophrenics showed a longer left square tracing than depressives (DSM III, only *P*<0.05). This lack of difference was not due to a lack of abnormal test performance in the sample as a whole since impairments were found and these showed strong relationships with the mental state abnormalities (Table 5.2), particularly between poorer test performance and worse negative symptoms. Strong relationships between poorer psychological test performance and worse positive symptoms were also established but many fewer tests were involved. It was not possible to explain the relationships with either positive or negative symptoms on the basis of neuroleptic ingestion as there was no difference in any test result between those off and on neuroleptics at the time of testing. There were no direct significant relationships between

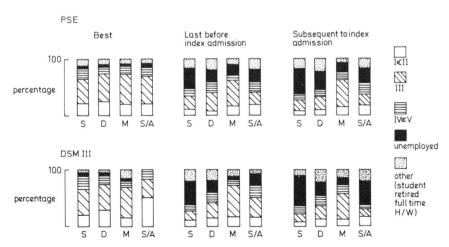

Fig. 5–3.   Best, last, and subsequent occupations (in terms of Registrar General's classification) of patients in various diagnostic categories in the follow-up to the 'Functional' Psychosis Study (Johnstone *et al.* 1992). S, schizophrenic; D, depressed; M, manic; S/A, schizoaffective.

Table 5–2 Relationships between psychological test results and positive and negative symptoms where significant, poorer performance is associated with worse symptoms)

Psychological test	Mean Score of:				Significance (P)
	+ve ≤1; −ve ≤1	+ve ≤1; −ve ≥2	+ve ≥2;−ve ≤1	+ve ≥2; +ve ≥2	
DSST	10.3	8.5	8.8	7.3	+ve (<0.001) −ve (<0.0001)
Memory	5.7	4.8	5.5	4.9	−ve (<0.01)
NART	108.7	107.9	108.1	101.5	−ve (<0.05)
Comprehension	11.4	9.2	10.8	8.1	−ve (<0.01)
Similarities	11.4	9.1	10.7	8.5	−ve (<0.01)
Block design	10.4	8.9	9.7	9.0	NS
Picture completion	9.5	8.5	8.5	6.8	+ve (<0.01) −ve (<0.01)
Peg board right	−0.05	−0.06	−0.04	−0.03	NS
Peg board left	72.3	81.9	84.8	82.0	NS
Square tracing right	19.9	25.7	19.0	29.6	−ve (<0.001)
Square tracing left	9.5	13.9	9.6	12.0	−ve (<0.001)
Annett	10.7	10.7	10.5	10.0	NS

psychological test performance and either Montgomery–Asberg (1979) or Bech–Rafaelsen *et al*. (1978) score.

Consideration of clinical (mental state) occupational and treatment variables in this study showed that there was no measure in which a better outcome at 2.5 years was found in patients with an index diagnostic classification of schizophrenia than in other diagnostic groups and several in which, after this relatively short follow-up period, it was significantly worse. It could thus be concluded that outcome in these terms does indeed validate the distinction between schizophrenia and affective disorder. The lack of differences between the diagnostic groups in terms of the psychological tests fits in less well with this distinction. The lack of association between schizophrenic diagnosis and psychological test performance makes it clear that whatever is the reason for the occupational decline of the schizophrenic patients it is not simply the development of cognitive deficits. The cognitive deficits showed clear relationships with the abnormalities of the mental state present at the time of testing. Relationships with positive symptoms were found but in general the relationships with negative symptoms were stronger and more tests were affected. Although at least as far as DSM III classification was concerned negative symptoms were more common in patients with index classifications of schizphrenia and schizoaffective disorder they did occur in all diagnostic groups and it was with their presence and not with the diagnostic classifications that the impairments of psychological test performance are associated. Therefore, if it were to be considered as it has been (Ingvar 1987) that cognitive deficits are an integral part of the defect state which so cripples some sufferers from functional psychotic illness, then the diagnostic classifications which were used were a poor predictor of the development of that defect. In view of the fact that there is a significant association between the index diagnostic classifications and the development of negative features which are strongly associated with the cognitive deficits, the classifications cannot be said to be irrelevant to liability to cognitive impairment but there was no direct relationship. The historical and clinical variables which showed a significantly worse outcome for schizophrenic patients confirmed the value of outcome in validating Kraepelin's dichotomy of dementia praecox (1899) and manic-depressive insanity. On the other hand, the diagnostic classifications did not predict cognitive impairments which were found to be associated with concurrent mental state abnormalities.

Apart from acting as a guide to treatment the purpose of diagnosis is to predict the future course of a disorder. We might hope that diagnostic classification of functional psychosis would provide a prediction of which patients would be found to have the defect state characterized by negative symptoms and cognitive impairments which so cripples some of those who have had psychotic episodes and which may be considered a hallmark of schizophrenia. The classifications used were of little value in this respect. It was concluded that the part of the study which considered the usefulness of acute treatment response as a validating criterion for diagnostic categorization tended to support the symptom-dimensional rather than the diagnostic category approach to the characterization of psychopathology (Johnstone *et al*. 1988*a*). The results of the outcome section of the study are understandably less clear-cut but from the point of view of the psychological aspects these findings too would tend to favour the symptom-dimensional approach. This is a view of the psychopathology of psychosis which has received increasing recent support (Persons 1986; Attman and Jobe 1992).

6

Post-mortem studies of schizophrenia

The idea that schizophrenia may be associated with structural brain changes is as old as the concept of the disease and may indeed precede its clear definition. In 1891, Clouston wrote of central nervous system abnormalities as a feature of the disorder that he called adolescent insanity and later considered as included in Kraepelin's concept of dementia praecox. In 1896, Kraepelin defined dementia praecox, later known as schizophrenia. In 1907, with reference to this disorder, he stated: 'the fact is decisive that the morbid anatomy has disclosed not simple inadequacy of the nervous system but destructive morbid processes as the background of the clinical picture'. In spite of confident assertions of early workers in this field, nine decades of endeavour have not provided unequivocal evidence of these destructive morbid processes. Kraepelin's definition of dementia praecox was shortly followed by a histological study by Alzheimer (1897) in which he described cell loss and gliosis in schizophrenia. In 1924, however, Dunlap described an investigation in which three independent observers made cell counts of the cortical layers where changes in schizophrenia had been noted by Alzheimer and found no difference between schizophrenics and controls. Cellular changes similar to those which had been described in schizophrenia were found in both groups. This study cast lasting doubts over the field (David 1957).

The recent resurgence of interest in post-mortem studies of schizophrenia promoted by the findings of imaging studies has indicated that some structures in the schizophrenic brain are reduced in size (Bogerts *et al.* 1985; Jellinger 1985) and recent histological studies (Stevens 1982; Kovelman and Schiebel 1984; Jakob and Beckman 1986) have once again raised the possibility of glial changes and abnormalities of neuronal architecture in the brains of schizophrenic patients. A large retrospective clinico-neuropathological study was carried out by the Division of Psychiatry at the Clinical Research Centre on brains of patients who had died in Runwell Hospital (Brown *et al.* 1986). Schizophrenic brains were compared with those of patients with affective illness and it was found that they were significantly lighter and had significantly larger ventricles. This was a retrospective study and depended on casenote diagnosis. Reliance upon casenotes written in a variable style by many different people is less than satisfactory and adds to the difficulties of the post-mortem study of the schizophrenic brain. This is a field of investigation that will always have the problems which result from the heterogeneity of the condition, the lack of a diagnostic marker, and the very long time interval from the onset of the illness—usually in the third decade and death, which on average, is in the seventh decade. In those 40 years the brain may be subjected to a variety of insults and the mental state may fluctuate a great deal. It is likely that the clinical picture at death will be very different from that at onset or at the worst stage of the illness.

The prospective clinico-neuropathological study

The need for a prospective clinico-neuropathological study of schizophrenic patients who had been systematically studied and a control group of patients with no known psychiatric neurological illness became clear. It was evident to the staff of the Division of Psychiatry, Clinical Research Centre, Northwick park, that we were very well placed to perform such an investigation, because of the assessments which had been made in the 510 schizophrenic patients in Shenley Hospital for the inpatient survey (Owens and Johnstone 1980)

The investigation which was conducted (Bruton *et al.* 1990) was designed to examine both macroscopical and histological brain structure and also to assess whether there was sufficient neuropathological evidence to support any of the aetiological explanations which have been advanced to account for the structural abnormalities reported in the brains of schizophrenic patients (Stevens 1982; Murray *et al.* 1985; Roberts and Crow 1987). The sample was compared of 56 schizophrenic patients and 56 normal controls matched for age and sex. Thirty-eight of the schizophrenics were part of the sample of the inpatient schizophrenia survey of Shenley Hospital patients (Owens and Johnstone 1980). The need for patience in this area of work is underlined by the fact that it took 10 years for those 38 brains to be accrued even though the 510 patients from whom they were drawn were, on average, almost 60 years of age when the sample was identified. These patients had been examined several times during their lifetime in connection with various investigations (Owens and Johnstone 1980; Owens *et al.* 1982, 1985; Ferrier *et al.* 1983; Johnstone *et al.* 1987*a*). Historical information had been recorded in detail and clinical neurological and psychological status had been assessed in a standardized manner. All of these patients fulfilled the St. Louis criteria (Feighner *et al.* 1972) for schizophrenia and the Syndrome Check List of the Present State Examination (PSE) (Wing *et al.* 1974) had also been applied. Two further patients had been assessed in detail during their lifetime at Northwick Park Hospital and fulfilled the St. Louis criteria (Feighner *et al.* 1972) for schizophrenia. The remaining 16 patients died in other hospitals and had not been examined in a comparable way. Nevertheless, their casenotes were examined and the St. Louis criteria (Feighner *et al.* 1972) and the Syndrome Check List of the PSE applied to them. The 'normal control' group comprised cases of sudden death occurring in previously healthy individuals who lived in the catchment area of the Southend District Health Authority. Coroners' reports and general practitioners' records were checked to exclude people who were known to have suffered from any neurological or psychiatric disorder during their lifetime. Each brain was coded and later examined without knowledge of the clinical history. One half of each brain was deep frozen and the remaining half brain was fixed in formalin for histological examination (Bruton *et al.* 1990). The mean age at death for males (schizophrenics, 67.7 years; controls, 65.7 years) was 11 years less than that of the females (schizophrenics, 78.8 years; controls, 78.4 years).

At the end of the study when the neuropathological code numbers were combined with the clinical details, it was found that eight of the schizophrenic patients had additional neurological complications (Table 6.1) and they were removed from the study in order to keep both samples comparable. Both brain weight and brain length were significantly reduced in the schizophrenic as compared with the control brains ($P<0.001$ and $P<0.01$, respectively). After brain measurements had been made, detailed histological examination was carried out. There was no significant difference between schizophrenics or controls in the amount of vascular disease or in the presence of senile plaques and neurofibrillary tangles. There was, however, an excess of focal damage and other pathology in the schizophrenic brains as compared with the controls, and this was the case after removal of the eight patients with known neurological complications. Twenty-one of the 48 schizophrenics (44 per cent) had some degree of localized cerebral pathology compared with 12 of the 56 (21 per cent) control patients ($P<0.01$). This figure of 44 per cent is not dissimilar from the 50 per cent reported by Stevens (1982) and the 51 per cent by Jellinger (1985). In our study the variety and localization of the damage could certainly be described as diverse. It included degeneration of the

Table 6–1 *Patients whose brains were removed from post-mortem study because of the development of neurological complications*

Leucotomy	3 cases
Terminal cerebrovascular accident	1 case
Initially Feighner positive cases who later developed neurological complications	4 cases (2 epilepsy; 1: Friedreich's ataxia; 1: multiple sclerosis)

substantia nigra, calcification of the hippocampus, a ganglioglioma of the pons, focal softening of the cerebellum, and infarction of the striatum. This diversity made it difficult to detect changes between the groups in the type of pathology and certainly it was not easy to see how these scattered and very different types of pathology could lead to a final common pathway by which they could have given rise to schizophrenic symptomatology. In this respect the interpretation of this study has similar difficulties to that of our study of underlying organic disease in patients with first schizophrenic episodes (Johnstone *et al.* 1987*h*).

The question of the presence of gliosis in the brains of schizophrenic patients has been controversial (Roberts *et al.* 1988; Stevens *et al.* 1988). The findings of this study did not greatly clarify this issue. There certainly was gliosis in both schizophrenic and control brains (Table 6.2) and while in both groups of subjects the presence of focal pathology was significantly associated with increased fibrillary gliosis in both the cerebral cortex and hemisphere white matter ($P<0.001$) there was no significant relationship between the presence of focal damage and increased levels of fibrillary gliosis in the periventricular structures. The cause of this periventricular gliosis is unclear. To determine if there was a direct relationship between cerebral gliosis and the reduced brain size in terms of brain weight, length and increased ventricular size all subjects whose brain showed histological evidence of significant Alzheimer-type change, cerebrovascular disease, and any form of focal pathology were removed from the analysis. This

Table 6–2 *Histological features in schizophrenic and control brains (after Bruton et al. 1990)*

Histological Features	Presence*	Schizophrenic group (n = 48)		Control group (n = 56)	
		Male	Female	Male	Female
Fibrous gliosis cortex	0	11	6	24	6
	1	13	6	7	15
	2 and 3	4	5	1	3
Fibrous gliosis white matter	0	5	2	10	3
	1	15	14	19	18
	2 and 3	8	4	3	3
Fibrous gliosis peri-ventricular structures	–	11	8	20	13
	+	17	12	12	11
Focal damage	–	18	9	25	19
	+	10	11	7	5

* 0, none; 1, slight; 2, moderate; 3, severe; –, absent; +, present.

produced a group of 18 schizophrenics and 22 controls. These 18 schizo-phrenic brains continued to show significant reduction in brain weight and length and increase in ventricular size when compared with controls but showed no evidence of increased gliosis. It was therefore concluded that the structural abnormalities of reduced brain length, reduced brain weight, and increased ventricular size could occur in the absence of increased levels of gliosis. The principal neuropathological findings of this study were therefore as follows:

In comparison with the brains of normal controls the brains of people who had suffered from schizophrenia showed brain weight reduced by 4.5 per cent and brain length reduced by 0.7 cm in men and 1 cm in women. Ventricular size was increased, there was an excess of non-specific focal pathology, and an excess of gliosis was detected. Gliosis of the cerebral cortex and white matter was highly significantly correlated with the presence of focal damage, but periventricular fibrillary gliosis was not. After exclusion of cases with Alzheimer change, cerebrovascular disease and focal pathology from the sample, the decrease in brain weight and length and the increase in ventricular size continued to distinguish the schizophrenics from the controls.

This was, of course, a clinical as well as a pathological study. The strong clinical data concerned the 38 schizophrenic patients who had been included in the initial survey of inpatients in Shenley Hospital (Owens and Johnstone 1980) many of whom had survived to be reassessed in connection with later studies (Owens *et al.* 1982, 1985; Ferrier *et al.* 1983; Johnstone *et al.* 1987a). The methods used for the mental state assessments were the same for all of the investigations and those used for the clinico pathological study were those conducted nearest to the patient's death (Johnstone *et al.* in press.). Five of these 38 patients were removed from the sample because they were among the eight who were excluded because they had developed super-added neurological complications. Three of these related to previous treatment (leucotomy) and one patient had suffered a terminal cerebrovascular accident. The remaining case, while working as a ballerina in a prestigious company, had developed a psychotic illness in the absence of detectable neurological abnormality and when she was first assessed at Shenley Hospital by staff from the Division of Psychiatry this illness fulfilled the St. Louis criteria for schizophrenia (Feighner *et al.* 1972). She later developed motor and cerebellar signs and post-mortem confirmed the diagnosis of multiple sclerosis. Therefore, 33 brains remained from patients with schizophrenia in whom substantial historical and clinical information was available. The historical information available included pre-morbid educational attainment, occupational and social functioning, family history of mental disorder, patients exposure to physical treatment in terms of insulin coma, electroconvulsive therapy (ECT), neuroleptics, and less common treatments such as cardiazol shocks, TAB (typhoid and paratyphoid A or B) vaccine, and dexedrine. We also had information on birth trauma and head injury, physical illnesses throughout life, and took note of unusual circumstances which could possibly have been relevant, for example, one patient had been an inmate of a displaced persons' camp at the end of the Second World War and another had given birth to two children who had serious central nervous system disorders. We also included in the analysis the last assessments that had been done of positive and negative symptoms, cognitive function, and movement disorder. Pathological data was considered in terms of brain weight and length and the presence of focal damage. It can be unequivocally stated that there was no evidence that birth trauma, head injury, physical illness throughout life, unusual circumstances or exposure to ECT, insulin coma treatment, or neuroleptics were related to the pathological findings (Johnstone *et al.* in press.). Lower brain weight and shorter brain length were significantly associated with impairments in terms of global function, cognitive function, and negative symptoms. There was also a significant relationship ($P<0.05$) between lower brain weight and poorer educational attainment. We cannot know whether this reflects a process specific to schizophrenia. It seems likely enough that such a relationship might be found in the general population, although appropriately collected information is not generally available. There were no relationships between focal damage and any historical treatment or psychopathological variable —its only significant association was with gender as it was significantly more likely to be found in women.

The aim of this part of the study was to relate the neuropathological findings which had been found in the sample of schizophrenic brains to the clinical details in the 33 patients who had been intensively studied during life. Although the heterogeneity of the clinical picture course and outcome of schizophrenia is well known this was not well represented in this sample. These brains came from patients whose illnesses were so severe that they had spent many years up until their deaths as long-stay inpatients even though active discharge and resettlement policies were in operation in the hospital where they lived at the relevant time. Clearly such a population is not ideal for this type of work but the difficulties of obtaining brains from well-studied patients who die out of long-stay hospitals and especially those whose deaths are unexpected and at a relatively young age are very great. Indeed, it has yet to be demonstrated that it is possible to get a sample of such brains that is large enough to be analysed. In spite of the homogeneity of the sample we were able to demonstrate significant clinico-pathological correlations. The clear negative findings were also of interest. The fact that it is clear that past physical illness, relatively minor head injury, treatment with ECT, insulin coma and neuroleptics, physical illnesses throughout life, or even exposure to circumstances of major deprivation did not have any bearing on the pathological changes means that in the future it will be easier to interpret findings from samples where these historical details are not known.

Interpretations of the findings

Various interpretations of the findings of this study are possible. Clearly, the reduction in brain weight and length and the increased ventricular size in the schizophrenic brains are fully compatible with the view that the brains of schizophrenic subjects contain visible and defined structural abnormalities that are of a developmental nature. The cause of such a developmental abnormality is unclear, indeed, there may be several causes—genetic factors are likely to be involved in at least some cases and early insults of various kinds are possible. These suggestions are speculative. There was no evidence relating to family history, birth trauma, or early history which offered any clues in this sample. Admittedly, there were only 33 cases and six or seven decades had passed since any relevant events might have taken place but very careful scrutiny revealed nothing. In addition to the structural abnormalities we did, of course, find focal histopathological damage which was almost certainly acquired. Our original interpretation (Bruton *et al.* 1990) was that schizophrenia is a developmental abnormality of the cerebral structure in which the structurally abnormal brain is excessively vulnerable to acquired damage in later life. Another, perhaps at least at first glance, more straightforward explanation is that schizophrenia is a final common pathway along which both developmental and acquired brain damage may become clinically expressed. The differing clinical correlates of the reduction in brain size and the focal damage strengthen the case for the latter hypothesis. These findings could be considered consistent with the view that there is a neurodevelopmental basis for schizophrenia in some cases but not others and that the neurodevelopmental form is common in males, more 'atypical schizophrenia-like' illness being more common in women (Castle and Murray 1991). In support of this view it is argued that male patients have an earlier onset, a poorer outcome, are more likely to exhibit poor pre-morbid adjustment, and to have structural abnormalities of the brain demonstrated by imaging techniques. Females, on the other hand, have a later onset (Lewine 1981; Hafner *et al.* 1989) and sometimes a more favourable outcome at least in social terms (Johnstone *et al.* 1981). The association of focal damage with the female sex would support the idea that when schizophrenia occurs in women it is sometimes on the basis of pathology separate from or additional to developmental factors. Such interpretation is in some ways appealing. It seems to make sense of various apparently unrelated pieces of information. It is, however, important to consider what acceptance of this interpretation would imply. It would mean that various diverse focal pathologies which can and do occur in persons who are evidently well are causative of schizophrenia in some people. Either this must mean that these focal pathologies which look the same are in fact different and that those which are associated with schizophrenia affect neural structures which are not involved in other cases, or it must mean that susceptibility to the effects of the focal damage varies in the population. This view has much in common with the idea that schizophrenia is associated with a structurally abnormal brain which is excessively vulnerable to acquired damage in later life. The study did not offer us any solid evidence about the cause of the reduced size of the schizophrenic brains. The periventricular gliosis is difficult to interpret. We could find no cause for it in our detailed historical information and reduced brain size occurred in the purified sample where it was not present (Bruton *et al.* 1990). We are left with speculations about genetic factors and early insults but in this investigation, at least, no clear evidence of either.

7

The 1975–85 cohort: a 3 to 13 year follow-up study

The need for a follow-up study of a representative sample of schizophrenic patients

Reference has already been made to the heterogeneity of schizophrenia. It is often at least tacitly assumed that patients who participate in investigations of the disorder from which they suffer are reasonably representative of the generality of persons with the same condition. As far as psychotic illnesses are concerned this assumption is unlikely to be justified. The patients in the large trials described in earlier chapters were highly selected—120 from 326 in the 'Functional' Psychosis Study and 120 from 462 (of whom 253 would have been suitable had they been prepared to be included) in the First Episodes Study. The patients in the large outcome studies were selected because they had been inpatients of a large mental hospital and in many cases had remained there for substantial periods. Although in general, the studies conducted at the Clinical Research Centre (CRC) had tended to suggest that the prognosis of schizophrenia remained very limited, some other authors (M. Bleuler 1978; Ciompi 1980; Harding *et al.* 1987) described a more optimistic outlook. Scrutiny of their work certainly allows the view that this difference is a matter of interpretation rather than findings. For example, M. Bleuler's criteria for recovery allow the persistence of delusions and perceptual disturbance (M. Bleuler 1978). Nonetheless, it seemed valuable to examine outcome in a large complete cohort of schizophrenic patients who had not been selected by their willingness to co-operate with studies, need for continued hospitalization, or any other such criterion.

At the time that this idea was considered there was both national (*Lancet* 1985) and local (NWTRHA 1985) concern about the advisability of policies of replacing psychiatric inpatient care with community care. There had, of course, been consideration of such policies in the United Kingdom for over 20 years (Tooth and Brooke 1961) and in the United States the plan of replacing inpatient care with care in the community was partially adopted (Scharfstein 1978; Fink and Weinstein 1979; Winslow 1979). In Italy it was carried out in a much more complete way at least in some areas (Jones and Poletti 1985, 1986) but problems appear to have arisen in both countries.

The matter of the advisability of policies of replacing inpatient psychiatric care with community care has been extensively discussed in the medical and national press in Britain. Some writers are generally supportive of the idea of community care (Sturt and Waters 1985) but grave disquiet about the welfare of discharged patients with serious mental disorders has been expressed by others (Weller 1985). Relatives' organizations and others concerned with patients' welfare have provided case reports which are extremely disturbing (NSF 1979; Wallace 1983). Strong opinions are expressed but they are often conflicting (*Lancet* 1985). Much of this difficulty and uncertainty relates to a lack of information about the long-term course and outcome of psychiatric illness, especially schizophrenia, which has been managed in different ways, and the unrepresentativeness of the samples used in the studies which have been done is only one of many problems.

The 1975–85 study

Against this background we decided to conduct a study (Johnstone *et al.* 1991) which had the aim of identifying, tracing, and examining in various standardized ways all schizophrenic patients discharged from inpatient and day patient services in Harrow between 1 January 1975 and 1 January 1985. It was our intention to examine the patients in terms of their mental state, cognitive functioning, extra-pyramidal function, and social disability; and to relate their current status in those terms to demographic, historical, and treatment variables. The patient sample consisted of all those fulfilling the St. Louis criteria (Feighner *et al.* 1972) for schizophrenia in definite or possible degree who were discharged between the above dates from inpatient or day patient care in the Psychiatric Unit, Northwick Park Hospital, or from wards in Shenley Hospital which admitted patients from Harrow. This sample consisted of 532 cases, 291 men and 241 women: 498 of these patients were successfully traced (Johnstone *et al.* 1991b). Not all were interviewed because some refused, some were abroad, and some were dead but the fact that 93.6 per cent were successfully traced does mean that the findings may reasonably be considered as representative of all schizophrenic patients discharged from these services over the decade 1975–85. It also means that the view which is sometimes expressed (Furlong 1987; Hammond 1987), that information about discharged schizophrenic patients will not be able to be obtained for reasons of geographical instability, lack of family contact, and unstable accommodation, cannot be sustained in this sample.

Harrow is not, of course, typical of the rest of the London area and certainly not of the United Kingdom as a whole. It is situated on the north-west perimeter of Greater London and is one of the wealthiest of the London boroughs. This is not because there is a high concentration of wealthy people—the grand part of the borough around the school, which includes Sir Winston Churchill among its many illustrious former pupils, is very small—but because it is an area of high owner-occupancy, low unemployment, and little local industry. Those residents who do not own their own homes are largely tenants of the local authority as there is very little accommodation in lodging houses, bedsitting rooms, or available for other forms of short-term rental. This means that the residents tend to be socially stable and thus easily traced either personally or through relatives. Many commute for employment into central London and others are blue-collar workers or are self-employed often in retail trade. Such circumstances are not rare in the towns and cities of Britain, particularly in the south, but inner cities are different in many ways and our experience in the First Episodes Study (Johnstone *et al.* 1986*b*) where a wide range of medical centres was used, suggests that we would have been unlikely to enjoy such success in tracing patients admitted from some inner London boroughs where many patients on admission had been living alone at temporary addresses.

The findings have been reported in substantial detail (Johnstone *et al.* 1991*b*) and only certain issues will be summarized or discussed here. Clearly, schizophrenia remains a very common disorder as over 500 individuals were discharged from this service over a 10 year period. Even though this is not strictly a catchment area population and the interest of the staff at CRC in schizophrenia is likely to have meant that patients with this condition would be to some extent diverted from other services, this large number is a clear indication of how frequently this disease presents. It was very apparent that in the majority of cases the illness is associated with recurrent or persistent problems. The mean number of admissions required over the follow-up period was 5.37 (Fig. 7.1) and, on average, patients spent 13.7 of the 120 months between 1975 and 1985 in hospital (Fig. 7.2). At the time of the follow-up interview, morbid levels of positive psychotic symptoms were present in about half of the sample and a maximum score on at least one positive symptom in about a quarter. Negative symptoms were less prominent. Symptoms not specifically associated with schizophrenia were also directly enquired for. Elevation of mood, irritability, and over-activity were rare and although tiredness, poor concentration, and depression were each described in over 40 per cent of cases they were rarely present in severe degree. Abnormalities of movement, especially bradykinesia, were frequent but again they were rarely severe. As in some previous studies by others (Garmezy 1978; Hemsley 1982; Morice 1990; Nelson *et al.* 1990) the patients in this study showed substantial impairments in IQ and, in many aspects, of cognition (Frith *et al.* 1991). There was no suggestion at all of a pre-morbid impairment in IQ at least in terms of those aspects of pre-morbid IQ measured by the NART (New Adult Reading Test) (Nelson and O'Connell 1978). This result goes against the notion that there is a subgroup of schizophrenic patients who were

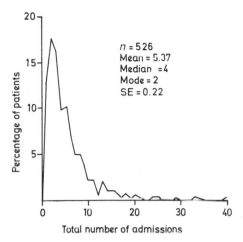

Fig. 7–1. Total number of admissions of schizophrenic patients in the follow-up period in the 1975–85 cohort study.

impaired from an early age (Harvey and Murray 1990). Rather, it suggests that schizophrenia can occur at any level of IQ. There was, however, a relationship between low pre-morbid IQ and subsequent symptoms. These patients had more severe features of schizophrenia, particularly negative features. Such patients also had a longer illness and were more likely to be inpatients. One consequence of these relationships is that any study in which the schizophrenic sample was restricted to inpatients and/or patients with negative features would find that they had low pre-morbid IQs. Such findings are likely to speak as much of the nature of the selection procedure as of the nature of schizophrenia. The relatively high pre-morbid IQ levels

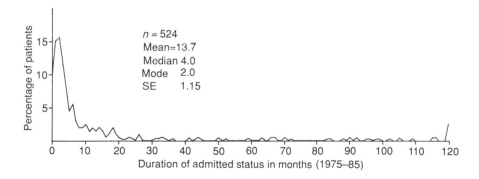

Fig. 7–2. Duration of admitted status of schizophrenic patients in the follow-up period in the 1975–85 cohort study.

found in the patients were paralleled by their pre-morbid occupations. At their best over 60 per cent had worked in occupations classed as social class 3 or higher, i.e. they had worked in a skilled or professional capacity (Table 7.1).

The occupational decline characteristic of schizophrenia (Goldberg and Morrison 1963) was clearly shown in this population. It was already evident in the last occupations held before the index admission (i.e. the first admission of that patient leading to discharge between 1975 and 1985) and at follow-up that further deterioration had taken place. At that time, only 19.7 per cent were in full-time work in any capacity (Leary et al. 1991). A further 11.8 per cent did part-time work, but 63.8 per cent were unemployed and less than 5 per cent of the total attended any kind of training programme, industrial therapy unit, day hospital, or day centre.

This lack of involvement in supportive social arrangements provided by the authorities was seen again when living arrangements were scrutinized (Table 7.2) Very few of the patients lived in hostels—indeed an even lower percentage than at the time of the earlier study (Johnstone et al. 1981). Although some of those recorded as living alone or in shared circumstances were in accommodation provided especially for mentally ill people by the local authority, in terms of individual flats or group homes this was by no means true of all in these categories. As far as accommodation was concerned most patients were dependent upon their own resources or those of relatives. Most patients, although fewer relatives, were reasonably satisfied with their living arrangements and, as in the earlier study (Johnstone et al. 1981), very few patients or relatives

Table 7–1 Best and last occupational levels of patients in the 1975–85 study

Social class (HMSO 1980)	Best* occupational level no. (%)	Last* occupational level no. (%)
1	4 (0.8)	2 (0.4)
2	54 (10.4)	25 (4.8)
3 (non-manual)	186 (36.0)	59 (11.4)
3 (manual)	78 (15.1)	26 (5.0)
4	69 (13.3)	43 (8.3)
5	46 (8.9)	43 (8.3)
Housewife	21 (4.1)	68 (13.2)
Unemployed	17 (3.3)	201 (38.9)
Other	42 (8.1)	50 (9.7)

* (Best, highest occupation held for one month or more; last, last occupation held before index admission, in terms of the Registrar General's classification (HMSO 1980).

Table 7–2 Patients' living circumstances

	1975–85 cohort (% patients)	1970–5 cohort (% patients)
Alone	24	11
Spouse/Cohabitee	25	33
Parents/Siblings/Children	34	38
Hostels/Residential	5	12
Shared/Lodgings	11	5

(less than 1 per cent of either group in this study) wanted the patient to return to hospital. This finding can certainly be interpreted as a very strong endorsement for community care policies on the part of both patients and relatives but it is also a clear indication that inpatient care is something that they wish to avoid. We would not expect or hope that patients would want to be admitted to hospital or that their relatives would wish to see them placed there. Nonetheless, the fact that so very few wanted a resumption of inpatient care in spite of the fact that some patients were quite ill when seen and about half of the relatives thought that there were ongoing problems, some severe, with the patient's condition, does suggest that efforts should be made to ensure that inpatient care becomes an experience that patients will be less unwilling to repeat.

It was clear that many patients continued to depend quite heavily on their relatives who on the whole were willing to accept an often considerable burden. The relatives of schizophrenic patients have sometimes been harshly treated by the psychiatric services. At one time, concepts of 'schizophrenic mothers' and 'double-bind' situations in the home received uncritical support. More 'fashionable' concepts of the role of high expressed emotion can be interpreted in a similar light and I have met many parents who rightly or wrongly have gained the impression that the staff caring for their schizophrenic child thought that the family's behaviour and attitude was in some way responsible for the patient's illness. It is very sad that the families of schizophrenic patients continue to feel that they are criticized in these ways as it was evident to me and all those involved in the large studies of schizophrenic patients living at home that the relatives of these patients cope with extremely distressing problems for long periods of time with very little support, and often at the cost of substantial personal sacrifice. The relatives interviewed in connection with this study gave graphic accounts of the social limitations experienced by the patients. These were categorized in various ways (Leary *et al.* 1991) but may be illustrated by the fact that more than 20 per cent of patients had not had any visitors to see them at their home in the previous six months, almost 14 per cent had not gone shopping at all for any purpose in the past month, even to buy a newspaper or a packet of cigarettes; and 44 per cent had not attended any place of entertainment in the past month. Our criteria for places of entertainment were set low so that this 44 per cent of the sample had not been in a cafe, public house or restaurant, even to have a cup of tea; a cinema, club, church or any place of entertainment or social contact for any purpose in the past month. From the relatives' account half of them lacked interest in current affairs and 60 per cent had no strong interest or hobby. In this area of work it is important not to allow one's view of the patient to be too much influenced by the standards of the relatively comfortably off bourgeoisie as represented by the medical profession. While bearing this in mind, the level of social impoverishment described above would surely be remarkable in any social class and at any income level.

As noted in Table 7.3 we were able in this study to compare and contrast the current findings with those of the earlier follow-up study of schizophrenic patients discharged from all Harrow beds (which at that time were in Shenley Hospital) between 1 January 1970 and 1 January 1975 (Johnstone *et al.* 1991). Striking aspects of the findings of that study were the uneven nature of the care which patients were receiving, the relatively high percentage of patients who were in contact with no aspect of the medical or social services (despite, in some cases, substantial disability), and the very considerable burden of care carried by the relatives. When the two cohorts were compared the first finding of note is the proportionally much larger number (532) of cases who were discharged between 1975 and

Table 7–3 *Patients' contact with services*

	1975–85 cohort (% patients)	1970–5 cohort (% patients)	Significance of difference between cohorts (P)
No medical or social support	5.8	27.2	<0.001
Contact only with community psychiatric nurse	2.7	12.6	<0.001
Contact only with GP	13.4	23	NS
Attending psychiatric clinic	45.4	16.6	<0.001
Attending more than one agency including psychiatric clinic	11.5	20	NS

1988 than between 1970 and 1975 (120 cases). This may reflect more active discharge policies but it is likely also to be due to the fact that Northwick Park Hospital, which has a district general hospital psychiatric unit and 12 national beds catering for mainly schizophrenic patients, opened in 1975. It may well be that patients were more willing to be admitted to a modern district general hospital located near to their homes than to a large mental hospital some distance away and, of course, the particular interest in schizophrenia of the staff at the Clinical Research Centre will have increased the number of patients treated locally for that disorder. The ages of the two samples were very similar. The contact with the services had been greatly improved by the time of the later survey (Table 7.3).

In spite of the greater degree of care including specialist care enjoyed by the patients in the later study there were no significant differences between the two samples with regard to the positive and negative features of their mental state. This was disappointing and raises the question of whether there is anything to be gained by the increased level of care given to the later sample. Examination of the findings relating to burden of care, however, makes it clear that the increased level of professional attention in the later study was associated with a substantial reduction in the concerns expressed by the relatives and certainly to those involved in the study, and in the relevant services this was an indication that their efforts were worthwhile (Table 7.4). Anxieties about the discharge of patients from long-term mental hospital care often include the concern that patients will become homeless and destitute, gravitate to prison, or die avoidable deaths. There was no evidence that schizophrenic patients discharged from Harrow services became homeless or destitute. Almost all of those traced had stable homes and although it is true that 6.4 per cent were not traced we know that these 34 cases include patients from circumstances which would ensure that they need never lack resources.

Certainly, there were avoidable deaths, 24 clearly unnatural (Anderson *et al.* 1991) (Table 7.5), but there was no evidence that the suicide rate was greater than that in the earlier sample, studied at a time when discharge policies were less active. Although open verdicts were recorded on 15 of the 24 unnatural deaths knowledge of the circumstances indicated that it was most unlikely that these deaths had been accidental. Those deaths occurred in patients aged between 21 and 60 years of both sexes, in those known to be floridly psychotic and in those believed to be in remission, in outpatients and in inpatients who included two under special observation for maximal suicide risk. As in earlier studies (Drake and Cotton 1986) and in our own other work (Johnstone *et al.* 1992) the highly educated were over-represented in the sample of patients who killed themselves. Fourteen of them had made previous attempts on their lives and some had made many such attempts. Some of those patients were well known to me and although, of course, I was not able to discuss their motivation at their final attempt

Table 7–4 *Burden of care of patients' relatives*

	1975–85 cohort (% of patients)	1970–5 cohort (% of patients)	P
Specific questions			
Time off work to look after patient	6.7	16	NS
Stopped work to look after patient	2.5	16	<0.001
Emotional illness in family*	16.8	13	NS
Physical illness in family*	9.2	6	NS
Social restrictions for family	30.8	48	NS
Additional items of concern			
No further worries	47.3	20	<0.01
Concern over future, particularly when relatives die	3.6	38	<0.0001
Distress over patient's evident suffering	0	10	–
Patient's dependence	7.6	13	–
Patient's loneliness	9.2	13	–
Patient's apathy/slowness	8.4	5	–
Fear of relapse	4.2	5	–

* Attributed by the relative to having the patient at home.

with them I was able to talk to a number of them at the time of their earlier attempts. I learned that while sometimes such attempts are driven by psychotic experiences other attempts, in the same individuals, result from a realization, while relatively well, of their own limitations, of how much they have lost and of how little the future holds for them. Much time and thought has been spent on the lessons that these deaths may bring but sadly it does not seem that they help us to devise any plan which will do a great deal more than perhaps postpone these unhappy events. The natural deaths include a statistical excess of deaths from cardiovascular disease especially in women. Reasons for this are unknown. Clearly avoidable deaths included a small number which obviously related to neglect which would not have occurred in people who were mentally well.

Very few of the patients in this study were found to be in prison or other judicial circumstances. At the time of the follow-up interview one man was

Table 7–5 Details of clearly unnatural causes of death

Verdict	Sex	Age (years)	Previous non-accidental	Inpatient at time of death	Details of death
Open					
	F	27	Yes	Yes	Drowning
	F	38	Yes	No	Impramine overdose
	F	42	Yes	No	Fell under train
	F	57	Yes	Yes	Drowning (in bath)
	F	60	Yes	Yes	Fell under train
	M	22	Yes	Yes	Fell under train
	M	23	No	No	Fell under train
	M	25	No	No	Fell under train
	M	26	No	No	Fell from balcony
	M	26	No	No	Orphenadrine overdose
	M	28	Yes	Yes	Fell under train
	M	31	Yes	No	Asphyxia with plastic bag
	M	33	No	No	Sodium amytal overdose
	M	37	No	No	Barbiturate overdose
	M	54	No	Yes	Fell under train
Suicide					
	F	21	Yes	Yes	Fell under train
	F	38	Yes	Yes (extended leave)	Hanging
	M	24	No	No	Hanging
	M	33	Yes	No	Jumped from high building
	M	34	No	No	Orphenadrine overdose
	M	38	Yes	No	Fell under train
	M	41	Yes	No	Asprin overdose
No inquest					
	F	39	Yes	Yes	Hanging
	F	45	Yes	No	Mixed overdose

in prison and three others were in special hospitals. We cannot, however, take this as evidence that the patients in this study were not coming into conflict with the law. Patients were directly asked about police contact since their discharge at the time of the follow-up interview. Just over 30 per cent of the sample had had contact with the police. Contacts were classed as: (a) neither charged nor convicted; (b) charged but not convicted; and (c) convicted. In the calculations which have been conducted each patient has been recorded only once under the most serious applicable category, i.e. if a patient was convicted on one occasion and charged, but not convicted on a second, he is recorded only under the convicted category. Thirty-eight patients had had contact with the police but had not been charged. Sometimes this contact resulted only from police involvement in their transfer to hospital or concerned the behaviour of their relatives. However, in some of the patients the behaviour bringing them into police contact could have led to charges and there was certainly no lack of evidence. An example of this is the fact that included in this category was a puerperal woman whose vulnerability was recognized and who was therefore under close supervision. She made a determined attempt to stab her baby son with a sharp knife in front of several professional witnesses. As in a number of other cases, charges were not brought because it was recognized that she was mentally ill and known that she had been admitted to hospital. Similar considerations apply to the 22 patients where charges were brought although there was no conviction. In general, it appeared that there was no lack of evidence but that charges were dropped because of the patient's mental condition and circumstances. Although many of the charges were relatively minor they did include assault, child abuse, possession of an offensive weapon, and attempted stabbing, arson and grievous bodily harm (one case each): 38 of the patients were convicted of offences and the nature of these is shown in Table 7.6. Apart from the driving offences, there were 10 convictions which concerned behaviour actually or potentially dangerous to others and some of them were very serious. It is important to consider whether and to what extent such behaviour is related to the mental illness of these patients and whether or not the risk of seriously dangerous behaviour can be predicted in individual cases. Information about the mental state at the time of the offence was not available in all of the cases in Table 7.6 but the patient who committed murder, the patient who attempted to murder her grandchild, and the patient who was convicted for grievous bodily harm, actual bodily harm and on three occasions for indecent assault all clearly acted under the influence of delusions. The grandmother believed that her grandson, a pre-school child, was possessed of a malignant and harmful force. This woman had had similar beliefs some years before about another grandchild of about the same age. The man who committed murder (of an African man whom he did not know, selected on the basis that he was the first Afro-Caribbean that he saw when he entered a railway station) did so on the basis of delusions about Afro-Caribbeans. This man moved away from Harrow about a year before the murder and I therefore did not see him during this time although he remained under psychiatric supervision and care from another hospital. At one time I knew him well and was very surprised by the murder. He was a small, unaggressive, rather dapper man. When floridly ill, his delusions concerned other topics and although he did have prejudices against Afro-Caribbeans I had not considered them to be other than those commonplace in members of his cultural background. I did not expect them to become incorporated into his delusional system or for him to act upon them in a violent way. The man convicted of grievous bodily harm, actual bodily harm and, on three occasions, of indecent assault has since died of unrelated natural causes. On the basis of recurring but treatable delusions about women, especially pregnant women, he had made repeated attacks against females whom he did not know. On maintenance neuroleptic treatment this patient was well and would agree that he required treatment. This assertion was not borne out in reality and those caring for him were extremely concerned that they had no legal power to enforce maintenance treatment for more than the short period after recovery that is now within the law.

Consideration of the rates of police contact in the group of patients as a whole in comparison with the normal population is not easy. There was an account of police contact before the index admission in 25 per cent of the entire sample and 30 per cent of those interviewed reported police contact in the follow-up period. Comparisons in rates of offending between the psychiatric patients and the general population is complicated by the need to correct for socioeconomic factors. McClintock and Avision (1968) compiled tables based on data for the year 1965 that estimate for the population of England and Wales the lifetime risk of appearing in criminal statistics. They estimated that the lifetime risk of conviction for any indictable offence was 29.5 per cent for males and 7.9 per cent for females. Higher rates than this have been reported for some groups of schizophrenic patients. Zitrin *et al.* (1976) found that 10 per cent of 403 schizophrenics were arrested for violent crime and 11 per cent for non-violent crime in the two years following their discharge from hospital. Some of these offenders were abusers of alcohol or drugs in addition to having schizophrenia. The rates of offending were below those of drug-dependent or alcoholic persons in the district and only slightly above the high rates of the general population in this catchment area. Nonetheless, Tidmarsh (1990) has reported that it has been considered that by publishing those results Zitrin *et al.* (1976) have brought discredit upon mentally ill people. The sufferers from schizophrenia are gravely disadvantaged and we would not wish to cause them any additional difficulties, but the rate of offending in this suburban population does give some cause for concern. It is anticipated that accurately matched figures for the general population will be able to be obtained which will allow appropriate comparisons to be made. However, in the meantime, the low rates of judicial custody in this sample should not be considered as evidence that active discharge policies for psychotic patients are not associated with rates of offending behaviour that should give rise to concern.

In summary, almost all patients in this up-to-date follow-up study of an unselected population of over 500 patients discharged with a diagnosis of schizophrenia were traced. Over 90 per cent of the patients were in contact with the medical services and many had continuing specialist supervision.

Table 7–6 *Offences of which patients were convicted*

Offence	No. of patients
Driving offences	
Speeding	2
Taking and driving away, and speeding	1
Taking and driving away, and drunken driving	1
Carrying a pillion passenger on a scooter	1
Driving without road tax and insurance	1
Driving without due care and attention	1
Offences actually or potentially dangerous to persons	
Assault of police and grievous bodily harm	1
Carrying an offensive weapon (a knife)	1
Attempted murder of grandchild	1
Grievous bodily harm, actual bodily harm, and three convictions of indecent assault	1
Assault of police	1
Attacked mother, causing actual bodily harm	1
Murder (stabbing to death of a stranger)	1
Assault of elderly woman	1
Theft, criminal damage, arson, and abandoning a dog in a flat	1
Threatening behaviour (repeatedly threatened to kill the child of a member of staff)	1
Offences against property	
Theft	5
Shoplifting	2
Possession of drugs	2
Fraud	2
Taking and driving away, and several breaches of the peace	1
Vagrancy	1
Shoplifting, trading without licence, begging, theft, fraud of Department of Health and Social Security	1
Criminal damage	1
Speeding, drunk driving, drunk and incapable	1
Breaking and entering	1
Theft and malicious damage	1
Breach of the peace	1
Theft, criminal damage, and vagrancy	1
Fraud and theft	1

Most received ongoing supervised anti-psychotic medication. In spite of this, in many cases the illness was clearly associated with recurrent or persistent problems. On the other hand, there were a few patients in whom the diagnosis seemed, even on review, to have been securely based but where recovery did appear to have taken place. One lady visited at home in the North of England just before Christmas had been out of hospital for years. She was a smiling, happy mother of three excited children. Her house was decorated for Christmas and she was awaiting the arrival of numerous family members for the holiday. She was symptom-free. Her level of function was obviously high and her mental state was completely normal. A second woman had also been well for years. She was a refugee from East Africa, the divorced mother of one son, who had her widowed frail mother living with her. She worked in a demanding capacity in a prestigious store in London's West End. She was symptom-free, socially charming, and with all of her responsibilities ran a very well-organized well-kept home with limited resources. These are striking examples of success but the outcome was very different for many. It has to be concluded that the general finding of most of our studies, that for the majority of schizophrenic patients the outcome remains limited in spite of maximal efforts at treatment, is supported by this study of a large unselected sample. Patient selection for the earlier studies does not really seem to have distorted the findings as far as outcome is concerned. Although it is difficult to find support in these findings for the optimism expressed by authors, such as M. Bleuler (1978), Ciompi (1980), and Harding *et al.* (1987), the nightmare scenario for discharged patients of homelessness, destitution, drift from care, illness, imprisonment, and death, invoked by other authors, most certainly was not applicable to these patients and on the whole they and their relatives did seem to have confidence in the services and to be reasonably pleased with the arrangements that had been made.

8

Schizophrenia and the National Child Development Study

The heterogeneity of schizophrenia in clinical presentation, outcome, and biological correlates, such as imaging and post-mortem findings, encourages the view that schizophrenia may be a disorder with more than one cause. This train of thought is not entirely logical as the heterogeneity of presentation, course, and final pathological picture of some disorders with essentially a single cause is proverbial, syphilis being a prime example, but in the last decade there has been a trend away from a search for a unifying characteristic of schizophrenia and towards the identification of differentiating characteristics (Lindenmayer and Kay 1992). While the cause or causes of schizophrenia remain unknown there is good evidence for a genetic contribution (McGuffin *et al.* 1987), although it seems highly unlikely that this is the sole causative factor (McGuffin 1990).

Perinatal events as causes of schizophrenia

Among possible non-genetic causes for schizophrenia perinatal events of various kinds have received recent attention. The finding that there is a slight excess tendency for schizophrenic patients to be born in the winter months of the year has been demonstrated by several groups (Dalen 1975; Hare and Walter 1978; Hafner *et al.* 1987). Whether this seasonality reflects an effect of temperature or other seasonal change is not known. Also, it is not known whether the critical influence occurs around the time of birth in the winter or perhaps early in the mother's pregnancy when, of course, the weather would be warm, but it is evident that a possible explanation for this finding would be that some form of damage to the infant occurring in relation to seasonal changes results in the later development of schizophrenia. Other findings which have increased interest in this area are those relating to reports of a considerable increase in rates of schizophrenia among second generation Afro-Caribbean immigrants (Harrison *et al.* 1988, 1989). There are a number of possible explanations for this effect including inappropriate diagnosis, inaccurate estimates of the ethnic distribution of relevant age groups of the population and the use of illicit substances by the affected samples. Nonetheless, a possible, although certainly unproven, explanation for increased rates of schizophrenia in this second generation immigrant population would be that the mothers of these individuals lacked immunity to viral infections endemic in the United Kingdom when they arrived here from the Caribbean in the 1950s and 1960s. It is known that such an effect did occur in relation to rubella and that these women gave birth to an excess of rubella-damaged children. It is possible that viral infection occuring at a particular time in pregnancy could be responsible for the later development of schizophrenia. This area of interest has been explored in relation to the influenza pandemic in 1957. It has been suggested that an excess of schizophrenia occurred in persons who were in utero at that time (Mednick *et al.* 1988). There has been evidence in support of this from some studies (O'Callaghan *et al.* 1991), but not others (Kendell and Kemp 1989; Bowler and Torrey 1990).

Apart from the question of seasonal and possible viral effects less specific damage occurring in the perinatal period has also been suggested as relevant to schizophrenia (McNeil and Kaij 1978; McNeil 1987; Eagles *et al.* 1990). There are difficulties in studying the relationship between perinatal events and the later development of schizophrenia largely because of the fact that this illness does not become evident until about 20 years after birth. Examining this relationship in established schizophrenics involves the scrutiny of past obstetric records which may be of very variable quality if they are available at all or else reliance upon the report of the mother who will, of course, not be blind to the fact that her child has developed schizophrenia. There is no means of knowing how this knowledge would affect the mother's recollection and report of events at the time of pregnancy and delivery 20 years before but it would be unwise to assume that it would have no effect. Indeed, detailed birth histories were taken from all available mothers of the patients in the 'Functional' Psychosis Study (Johnstone *et al.* 1988*a*) at the time of the follow-up interviews (Johnstone *et al.* 1992) with a view to comparing obstetric complications between the diagnostic groups. Significant differences were not demonstrated. I interviewed many of the mothers myself. I was impressed by the detailed accounts that they gave and it appeared to me that many of the mothers had clearly given much thought to the possibility that events at the time of the patient's birth might have been important for the later development of illness. They tended to present their account in polarized terms either describing the confinement as perfectly normal and the baby as entirely well or recounting problems and difficulties which objectively seemed to be fairly minor but which they felt to be very important. It is difficult to estimate the amount of distortion but it did seem to me that the accounts often lacked objectivity and, indeed, could mothers in that situation be expected to be objective?

Another method of considering the relationship between perinatal events and the later development of schizophrenia is to follow-up individuals affected by the events at birth which are thought to be relevant to later psychosis until the usual age of onset of schizophrenia. This type of strategy has most often been followed in individuals thought to be at high risk of schizophrenia because they are the children of schizophrenic mothers (e.g. Mednick and Silverton 1988). It could, in principle, be equally applied to babies affected by the type of perinatal event which is thought to be relevant but in both contexts the problem of the 20 year gap between birth and the development of the psychosis is a very considerable obstacle. This interval spans the effective working life time of many research workers. Methods of assessment are altered and updated with the passage of time and it is very difficult to maintain contact and interest over such a long time.

The combined use of the National Child Development Study data and the Mental Health Enquiry

An opportunity of overcoming these difficulties arose from the possibility of combining findings from two large, nationally collected sets of data. Great Britain has a unique tradition in conducting longitudinal birth cohort studies. Three continuing studies have been attempted, starting in 1946 (National Study of Health and Development), 1958 (National Child Development Study), and 1970 (British Cohort Study). Each was launched as a perinatal mortality survey of the 16 000 to 18 000 births occurring nationwide in a target week in 1946, 1958, and 1970. The study with which we are concerned here is the 1958, National Child Development Study (NCDS), the population of which comprised about 16 980 births registered with a birth date during the week 3 to 9 March 1958 representing 98 per cent of all births in England, Scotland, and Wales in that week. At that time the stillbirth and neonatal mortality rate was 35/1000 births; one of the main purposes of the study was to examine social and obstetric factors concerned with such deaths and a good deal of detailed information about the pregnancy, confinement, and neonatal period was collected. The second large nationally collected set of data with which we are concerned is the Mental Health Enquiry. This was set up in 1974 and recorded data including date of birth on all psychiatric admissions between 1974 and 1986. It occurred to the staff of the Division of Psychiatry, the Clinical Research Centre, Northwick Park, that from this source it would be possible to identify the records of every patient with a date of birth between 3 March 1958 and 9 March 1958 (and therefore every member of the NSDS cohort) who had been admitted to psychiatric care between 1974 and 1986. It would thus be possible to trace those members of the cohort who had developed schizophrenia and whose birth details would have been recorded in depth at the time they were born in the same way as all members of the cohort. It would be possible to compare the birth details of those who went on to develop schizophrenia with the rest of the cohort. This project was successfully conducted (Done *et al.* 1991). The tapes of the Mental Health Enquiry were scrutinized and 698 admissions representing 252 individuals were identified. In four cases, the clinician responsible refused permission and 17 sets of casenotes were irretrievably lost but 235 sets of casenotes were obtained and were examined in detail. Relevant aspects of the history were recorded and the syndrome check-list of the Present State Examination (PSE) (Wing *et al.* 1974) was applied to the notes. The diagnoses in terms of the categorization provided by the CATEGO programme are shown in Table 8.1 (Wing *et al.* 1974).

In the calculations, we assumed (as indeed did the retrospective studies) that the nature of any prenatal or perinatal events responsible for the later development of schizophrenia would be the same as those responsible for stillbirth and neonatal death. In the main analysis we did not find evidence in support of the suggestion that some schizophrenic illnesses are a result of birth trauma or high-risk pregnancy, when either a narrow or a broad diagnosis based on the PSE was adopted. There was also no support for the notion that there was a small group of schizophrenic patients who had an exceptionally risky gestation or birth. However, an increased prevalence of cases with a high risk was found in the group of patients with affective psychoses. The large group of neurotic subjects did not differ from the control groups. Once the main analysis was complete we considered the possibility that the variables relating to stillbirth and neonatal death might differ from those relating to the adult development of psychosis. We thus conducted an exploratory analysis involving a very wide range of maternal variables (Done *et al.* 1991). This analysis isolated specific risk variables associated with each diagnostic category. The variables associated with schizophrenia were lower maternal weight and the prescription of 'other drugs' to the baby (these were in fact antibiotics given for septic conditions

Table 8–1 *CATEGO Categorization of cases recorded by the Mental Health Enquiry with date of birth between 3 and 9 March 1958*

	S+/S?	*P+/P?*	*O+/O?*	*M+/M?*	*D+/D?*	*R+/R?*	*N+/N?/X*
Total	49	10	20	15	9	20	93
Born abroad	8	3	4	3	2	3	3
Otherwise unusable	6	0	1	2	0	2	14
Included in study	35	7	15	10	7	15	76

S+/S?, schizophrenia; *P+/P?*, paranoid; *O+/O?*, other psychosis; *M+/M?*, mania/hypomania; *D+/D?*, depression; *R+/R?*, retarded state; *N+/N?/X*, neurotic disorder.

to two children of schizophrenic mothers). The variables associated with affective psychosis were shorter duration of gestation (by 7.3 days) and the prescription of Synkavit (a fat-soluble form of vitamin K) to the baby. For neurotic illness the only variable approaching significance was bleeding during pregnancy. It is difficult to assess the meaning of these relationships and, of course, causality cannot be implied. Our conclusion from this study is that on their own, the findings in the schizophrenic patients can be taken as providing evidence against a role for early brain injury as an aetiological factor in schizophrenia. The findings on affective patients raise a number of questions. We cannot know what a standardized interview (rather than a casenote review) might have revealed or what diagnostic picture these cases of affective illness of early onset may finally show. Perhaps affective illness is truly associated with reduced mean gestation time or other perinatal anomaly, possibly some of the affective patients will turn out later to have schizophrenia—they certainly would not be the first schizophrenic patients whose illness, for whatever reason, was initially considered to be affective. We did however conclude that if there is an effect of perinatal trauma on the later development of psychotic illness it is weak, difficult to define, and apparently absent in typical schizophrenia of early onset.

The timing of the NCDS was fortunate in a way that could not possibly have been anticipated when it was designed. It has been considered that maternal influenza during pregnancy could be one of the environmental effects which might account for the season of birth effect in schizophrenia. In 1957, there was a pandemic of A2 influenza. Studies have been conducted to see whether or not there was an increased risk of schizophrenia in those who were in their second trimester of fetal life at the peak of epidemic. Some studies (Mednick *et al.* 1988; O'Callaghan *et al.* 1991) have found such an increase but others have not (Kendell and Kemp 1989; Bowler and Torrey 1990). The relevant birth week for the NCDS is 3 to 9 March 1958. Persons born then were in the second trimester of fetal life at height of the 1957 influenza epidemic which in Britain was between mid-September and mid-October of that year. In the NCDS, the question of whether or not mothers had had influenza during pregnancy was documented on the basis of an interview with the mother by the midwife who was also required to consult medical records relating to the pregnancy. We were thus able to compare notes of the subsequent development of schizophrenia in the children of mothers who had a history of influenza in pregnancy with those in children of mothers who had no such history (Table 8.2). Thus, although the influenza epidemic did reach a peak during the second trimester of the pregnancies of the NCDS mothers so that 945 mothers (5.8 per cent of the sample) were affected, only one child had later schizophrenia as defined by narrow diagnostic criteria and three children by a broader definition. These figures are closely comparable with the rates in children of non-infected mothers and with population expectation (Crow *et al.* 1991*a*).

Table 8–2 *Infection with influenza of the mother in pregnancy in relation to Subsequent psychiatric illness in the child*

Diagnosis	Total	No maternal influenza	Maternal influenza in trimester			
			1 (%)	2 (%)	3 (%)	P
Controls	16 179	14 153	231 (1.4)	945 (5.8)	675 (4.2)	NS
Psychoses	89	75	1 (1.1)	8 (9)	5 (5.6)	NS
Broad schizophrenia	57	50	0	3 (5.3)	4 (7)	NS
Narrow schizophrenia	34	30	0	1 (2.9)	3 (8.8)	NS
Affective Illness	32	25	1 (3)	5 (16)	1 (3)	NS

The follow-up of the NCDS sample

The NCDS sample was traced in 1965 (aged 7), 1969 (aged 11), and 1974 (aged 16). Parents were interviewed by a health visitor and tests were carried out by the local education medical officer. Currently, the findings of those assessments in those who went on to develop schizophrenia or affective psychosis are being compared with a 10 per cent sample of those who remained psychiatrically well (1500 controls). The study is complex and is not yet complete but the following significant findings have been made (Crow *et al.* 1991*b*). Individuals who will later suffer from schizophrenia or affective psychosis develop normally with respect to height, weight, and the onset of puberty. On the measures of social adjustment used, schizophrenics-to-be are hostile to adults and children and show 'inconsequential behaviour' at the ages of 7 and 11 years. Affective psychotics-to-be (but not schizophrenics) are rated restless at age 7 (but not 11) years and schizophrenics-to-be (but not depressives) are rated depressed at age 11 years. Schizophrenics-to-be manifest a wide range of deficits in reading and speech difficulties at the ages of 7, 11, and 16 years. Although not abnormal on a number of indices of a co-ordination at the ages of 11 and 16 years and vision tested at 11 years, schizophrenics-to-be are slow to develop continence and show poor physical co-ordination and vision at age 7 and clumsiness at age 16 years. It was concluded from this that schizophrenia is not a disorder of physical or sexual development, but that in at least some of those who develop this condition abnormalities of aspects of the functions of the nervous system, including reception and communication of language and development of social relations, are evident in early childhood.

9

Additional 'fashionable' themes in schizophrenia research

Genetic aspects

The genetic aspects of psychotic disorders have been the focus of considerable attention in the past few years. The idea that mental disorders run in families is a very old one and after defining dementia praecox, Kraepelin (1907) expressed the view that 'defective heredity is a very prominent factor'. The familiality of schizophrenia received continued investigation (Falconer 1965; Slater and Tsuang 1968) and in an elegant series of studies (Rosenthal *et al.* 1971; Kety *et al.* 1975) it was demonstrated that this familial tendency to develop the disorder was due not to shared environment but to shared genetic material. It was demonstrated that children removed from their biological parents at birth were at significantly greater risk of the later development of schizophrenia if there was schizophrenia among their biological relatives but not among their adoptive relatives.

Genetic studies of schizophrenia and indeed in mental illness generally have received a major impetus from the recent advances that there have been in molecular genetics. Prior to the development of these methods human linkage investigations were severely hampered by the poverty of informative markers in any given family. Until the advent of modern molecular genetics the markers that were used were restricted to those such as human leucocyte antigen system (HLA) or blood group polymorphisms. The use of restriction endonucleases has uncovered a considerable amount of previously inaccessible genetic variation. This variation, detected by restriction, fragment length polymorphisms (RFLPs) has dramatically increased the number of potentially informative markers in any given pedigree. The success of RFLP linkage methods in locating the loci for several important Mendelian disorders, most notably Huntington's disease, Duchenne's muscular dystrophy, and cystic fibrosis, has given great encouragement to molecular geneticists (Kendler 1987). There are two main approaches to linkage studies: one involving 'candidate' genes and the other a random search. Candidate genes are loci with known gene products where there may be a prior reason to suspect that the gene product is involved in the pathophysiology of a disorder. The major goal of linkage studies is to test the hypothesis that within a pedigree a given allele at the candidate locus is associated with the disorder. In the random research method probes are used to 'sweep' adjacent areas of the chromosome in an attempt to detect a locus of major effect. In the late 1980s there was a strong tide of enthusiasm and optimism about the possibility of finding genetic linkage for schizophrenia and manic-depressive psychosis. This enthusiasm has been tempered by the fact that initial positive findings have not been replicated. For example, it was reported that there was linkage between schizophrenia and the long arm of chromosome 5 (Sherrington *et al.* 1988) but subsequent studies did not replicate this (Kaufman *et al.* 1989; Kennedy *et al.* 1988; St. Clair *et al.* 1989). In a similar way, a linkage of manic-depressive illness in a large Amish family to a region of chromosome 11 (Egeland *et al.* 1987) was not supported by subsequent work (Kelsoe *et al.* 1989). It is difficult to know whether the original finding by Sherrington *et al.* (1988) represents a true genetic linkage or a falsely positive finding (De Lisi 1992) but certainly the vast publicity that there has been for positive findings in this field which were shortly followed by non-replication has not helped its credibility. A number of other suggestions for chromosomal linkage for schizophrenia have emerged but none has yet received firm support (De Lisi 1992).

It should be acknowledged that there are particular difficulties in the study of the genetics of mental disorders. Schizophrenia is a complex disorder of unknown aetiology. The boundaries of the phenotype are not known. The age of onset is in adult life and is variable. This is a very different situation from that pertaining, for example, to cystic fibrosis where the pathophysiology is understood, there is laboratory support for the diagnosis and the affected can be differentiated from the unaffected in early childhood. In spite of the difficulties, the fact that there is clear evidence of genetic vulnerability to schizophrenia together with the development of new technology which will allow, if perhaps in the fullness of a good deal of time, a systematic search of the human genome, does suggest that this is an area which merits continued support and investigation. Clinical studies do, however, indicate that it is by no means every case of schizophrenia in which a familial tendency can be detected. In the study of all schizophrenic patients discharged from Harrow beds between 1975 and 1985 (Chapter 7 and Johnstone *et al.* 1991*b*), all relevant casenotes were scrutinized for information on family history and a family tree was drawn up with a patient and with a relative, and each member discussed. The majority of cases had no obtainable history in either first or second degree relatives of schizophrenia or indeed of psychotic illness more generally (Table 9.1).

Not all of the patients were in close touch with their relatives, some of them came from very small families where it would be difficult to detect a familial tendency, and sometimes a family history of mental illness is concealed not only from doctors but also from other family members. I am aware of a small number of cases where this undoubtedly took place. In one the paternal grandmother of a patient told me that although she

Table 9–1 *History of psychotic illness in relatives of schizophrenic patients (Johnstone et al. 1991b)*

	Schizophrenia	Psychosis NOS
No. of relatives affected	435	403
Parent affected	22	57
Child affected	5	2
Sibling affected	35	24
Other relative affected	21	35
Uncertain	3	

had for nearly 40 years claimed to be a widow she did in fact visit her husband in a mental hospital every month. While her son knew his father to be alive and psychotic, his wife believed that her father-in-law had died before the Second World War and she had no knowledge that he had ever been mentally ill. The negative family history that she gave to me was therefore one that she believed to be accurate. It is probable that there are other instances of this kind but it seems very unlikely that such deceptions are widespread and it certainly seems possible that a genetic vulnerability to schizophrenia occurs in some families and not in others.

Dopamine receptors and atypical anti-psychotics

Genetic linkage is not the only aspect of research into the biological aspects of schizophrenia for which molecular biology is relevant. The antagonism of central nervous system D_2 receptor function by neuroleptic agents has been central to theories of the mechanism of anti-psychotic action of these drugs. Our understanding of dopaminergic function in the brain has been enhanced by molecular cloning of subtypes of the dopamine receptor. The subtypes include D_1 and D_2, together with three new receptors which have been labelled D_3, D_4, and D_5. The molecular cloning and characterization of the D_3 receptor was reported by Sokoloff *et al.* (1990), and the cloning of the D_4 receptor by Van Tol *et al.* (1991), and that of the D_5 receptor by Sunahara *et al.* (1991). The D_3 receptor was found to be localized in certain limbic areas of the brain. The generality of dopamine antagonist drugs show higher affinity for D_2 than D_3 receptors; 'atypical anti-psychotics', such as clozapine, however, appear to show a less marked preference for D_2 receptors over D_3. Clozapine, like other 'atypical anti-psychotics', has various mechanisms of action and which of these underlies the anti-psychotic effect is not yet known but certainly the cloning of these additional dopamine receptors opens promising avenues of enquiry. The D_4 receptor gene was reported to be highly homologous to the D_2 and D_3 receptor genes. Similarly, the pharmacological characteristics of this receptor resembled D_2 and D_3 receptors, with the difference that the affinity of the D_4 receptor for clozapine was found to be greater than that of the D_2 or D_3 receptor. It may well be that the recognition and characterization of this site will prove useful in the design of new neuroleptic agents. (Van Tol *et al.* 1991) The D_5 receptor has a similar pharmacological profile to the D_1 receptor but a much greater affinity for dopamine (Sunahara *et al.* 1991). The recognition and characterization of these additional dopamine receptors are very recent developments and at the present time it is not possible to say just what their implications will be but it is likely that selective ligands for these receptors will be sought. The finding of such ligands could well lead to the development of novel drug treatments for schizophrenia and if these were effective new light might be shed upon the relationship between schizophrenia and neurotransmission.

Although the demonstration of these new dopamine receptors is clearly relevant to the study of the mechanisms of action of 'atypical anti-psychotic agents' enhanced interest in these drugs preceded the finding of D_3, D_4, and D_5 receptors. There is no clear definition of the use of the term 'atypical anti-psychotic drugs' (Nutt 1990). The concept has been used to describe compounds that may differ in pre-clinical models or have atypical clinical effects (e.g. not elevating prolactin, not producing extra-pyramidal effects). The concept has also been applied to compounds that are more selective in their dopamine D_2 antagonist properties (e.g. sulpiride or raclopride) and/or have a broader range of effects upon neurotransmission and thus have marked anti-serotoninergic, anti-noradrenergic, or other effects, e.g. clozapine. In general, the criteria for characterizing a compound as atypical have not been reliably applied or well validated but they have served the purposes of helping to stimulate attempts at the development of new drugs that might possess novel clinical profiles. Clozapine, often used as the prototype of an atypical anti-psychotic drug was originally selected for further study in the hope that it might produce fewer extra-pyramidal side-effects than conventional neuroleptics (Meltzer and Fang 1975). This hope was realized and it was found to be effective in schizophrenic patients, particularly in the more severely ill (Fischer-Cornelssen and Ferner 1976), but its use was curtailed by the fact that its administration was associated with the development of agranulocytosis, although only in a small percentage of cases (Griffith and Saameli 1975). The suggestion that this drug may be useful in treatment-resistant cases has led to its further use. A trial conducted by Kane *et al.* (1988) showed that it had significantly greater benefits than chlorpromazine for treatment-resistant cases. The mechanism by which clozapine produces this effect is currently not known. An atypical anti-psychotic agent which does not produce agranulocytosis would clearly be highly desirable. Such compounds are under intensive investigation by the pharmaceutical industry and there is preliminary evidence that some of these, e.g. risperidone (Cartelao *et al.* 1989; Gelders *et al.* 1990) and melperone (Meltzer 1991) are effective anti-psychotics but none of them has really as yet been fully evaluated from the point of view of efficacy, safety, and relevant mechanism of action. If indeed they are found to be safe and effective, demonstration of their relevant mechanism of action may cast further light upon possible abnormalities of neurotransmission in schizophrenia.

Functional imaging

Psychopharmacology is not the only way in which neurotransmission in schizophrenia is investigated in life. It can be investigated with functional imaging. Positron emission tomography (PET) was, until very recently, the most powerful and practicable of functional imaging techniques. The processes which can potentially be studied with PET are numerous and are limited only by considerations of appropriate tracer design. The main processes which have been under investigation are: (a) cerebral blood flow, glucose, and oxygen consumption; and (b) neuroreceptor density and affinity—those are estimated using ligands such as ^{14}C-raclopride (Farde *et al.* 1990). It is likely that the development of further specific ligands will be a valuable tool in the monitoring of treatment and in the targeting of individual receptors. Early studies using PET demonstrated relative hypofrontality or reduced glucose metabolism in the frontal lobes sometimes correlated with negative symptomatology or neuropsychological impairment (Bench *et al.* 1990). PET can quantify tracer concentrates in absolute units. The measurement of the physiological or other variable can be expressed in absolute terms so that measurements made, e.g. within patient groups, are comparable. This capability is not available to the simpler and less expensive technique of single photon emission tomography (SPET) which can be used to measure relative cerebral blood flow and metabolism within different areas of the brain in one individual. Recently, cognitive challenge studies have provided an exciting impetus to neuropsychology. Appropriate use of tests may reveal and (with the concomitant use of PET and SPET) localize dysfunctional cognitive processes specific to certain psychiatric states including schizophrenia (Posner *et al.* 1988). At present PET studies of this sort are serving to underpin neuropsychological inferences but they are not necessarily increasing our understanding of the pathophysiology of the major psychiatric disease.

The success of PET studies has provided a stimulus for the development of functional magnetic resonance imaging. At present this is a very new development and studies so far are scanty (Belliveau *et al.* 1991). The method depends upon blood volume and susceptibility effects regionally within tissues. It is thought to provide a signal equivalent to the blood flow signal of ^{15}O PET with higher spatial resolution freedom from radiation exposure and in principle the possibility of an infinite number of repeat examinations in a single subject. This provides a great potential advantage over PET and SPET where the number of investigations which can be done in a single subject is strictly limited because of radiation issues. No formal studies on psychiatric patients of any kind have been published at the time of writing and the advantages and disadvantages in practice have yet to be determined.

Glutamate and schizophrenia

Although theories relating to dopaminergic transmission have dominated neurochemical studies of schizophrenia there is some evidence that suggests that impaired function of glutamatergic neurones might be aetiologically related to schizophrenia based on the psychotomimetic effects of phencyclidene, PCP ('angel dust') (Luby *et al.* 1962). The PCP receptor was described in 1979 (Zukin and Zukin 1979) but in 1990 studies established that the PCP receptor represents a site located within the ion channel formed by the *N*-methyl-D-aspartate (NMDA) receptor complex (Javitt and Zukin 1990). Agents that bind to the PCP receptor act as non-competitive inhibitors of the NMDA receptor complex, leading to disturbances of glutamatergic neurotransmission. It is thought that the abilities of PCP and other NMDA receptor antagonists to induce dopamine-like behaviour without primarily altering dopamine release may relate to the behaviourally antagonistic interaction between glutaminergic and dopaminergic systems in subcortical structures (Zukin and Javitt 1992). The ability of PCP acting as a non-competitive NMDA-receptor antagonist to induce schizophreniform psychosis suggests that endogenous dysfunction or dysregulation of NMDA receptor-mediated transmission might contribute to symptom generation in schizophrenia. The major neurotransmitter responsible for the activation of NMDA receptors is glutamate. In 1980 Kim *et al.* reported that glutamate levels were decreased in the cerebrospinal fluid of schizophrenic patients compared with controls, but other studies (Perry 1982; Gattaz *et al.* 1982) have not replicated this. Increased binding of kainic acid (Toru *et al.* 1988) and of [^{3}H] MK-801 (Kornhuber *et al.* 1989; Deakin *et al.* 1989) has been detected in specific brain regions of post-mortem schizophrenic samples suggesting that increased densities of both non-NMDA and NMDA receptors occur in specific brain regions. It has been suggested that the increased kainic acid binding might represent a compensatory response to impaired glutamate release (Toru *et al.* 1988; Deakin *et al.* 1989). Studies in this field have been few and it is not yet clear that they will be replicated but the area does merit further study. The difficulties of obtaining appropriate samples of schizophrenic post-mortem brain which have previously been mentioned are clearly relevant.

Social research in schizophrenia

This chapter has dealt with currently 'fashionable' areas in research in schizophrenia which have not been covered in earlier chapters. The issues mentioned have been clearly in the area of biological rather than social research. This reflects my own bias but is also a reflection of the balance of current interest in the different areas of research in schizophrenia—this has swung substantially towards biological issues in the last few years especially since the development of molecular genetics. There has however continued to be interest of 'expressed emotion' (EE). A number of social factors are known to be associated with exacerbations of positive symptoms in schizophrenic patients. A series of studies conducted by Wing and co-workers in the late 1950s and early 1960s, and reviewed recently by Wing (1989) showed that strong and unrealistic pressure to perform to high occupational and social standards was likely to precipitate relapse. Life changes of various, and not necessarily negative kinds, were also associated with relapse (Brown and Birley 1968). Later work has concentrated on the concept 'high expressed emotion' which is most simply operationalized in terms of critical comments made by some key relatives (Wing 1989). This concept has been studied in relation to and considered relevant for the prognosis of a wide range of disorders including depression, eating disorders, and inflamatory bowel disease. A number of studies in a variety of cultural settings have demonstrated a significant association between high EE and schizophrenic relapse (Brown *et al.* 1972; Vaughn and Leff 1976; Vaughn *et al.* 1984; Karno *et al.* 1987; Leff *et al.* 1987; Tarrier *et al.* 1989), although there are some studies where the association is less clear (Macmillan *et al.* 1986*b*; Dulz and Hand 1986; McCreadie and Robinson 1987; Parker *et al.* 1988). Studies of educational support and therapeutic groups (Leff *et al.* 1989; Tarrier *et al.* 1989) have usually but not always (Kottgen *et al.* 1984) indicated that it is possible, by family intervention of this kind, to reduce or at least delay relapse in vulnerable cases (Tarrier *et al.* 1989). Not all families, however, are willing to co-operate with such management and indeed those who seem most in need may be least willing to co-operate (Leff *et al.* 1989). Some studies have shown relatively few schizophrenic patients to be living with relatives who exhibit high EE (Macmillan *et al.* 1986*b*; McCreadie and Robinson 1987). In our own study at Northwick Park (Macmillan *et al.* 1986*b*), 81 of 253 patients lived alone, 36 were of unassimilated immigrant background and could not be assessed for EE, others refused and some were not discharged from hospital within the relevant time period. Thus the 77 patients where EE was assessed represent only 30.4 per cent of the initial eligible sample. Although 41 of the 77 families were assessed as sharing high EE, in only 6 of these was the patient in high social contact with the relevant family member. It is the combination of high social contact and high EE which has been thought to be associated with increased risk of relapse. It seemed fair to conclude from this study that even if this constellation of social factors is detrimental to schizophrenic patients it is unlikely to play an important role in a high proportion of cases.

10

Current knowledge and future plans

It is almost 100 years since the disease concept which came to be known as schizophrenia was defined (Kraepelin 1896). Detailed and careful studies of many aspects of the disorder have been conducted throughout this period and, particularly in the last 30 years, many worthwhile findings have been established. There have, however, been many inconsistencies and uncertainties. The key finding of the biological basis of schizophrenia—the structural or functional abnormality that is reliably found in most schizophrenics and not in other people and which will enable us to understand the pathogenesis of this tragic disorder is yet to be made. In nearly all of the studies described in the earlier chapters the tendency is to demonstrate findings that are true of some schizophrenic patients and not others and that are sometimes, although less often, found in patients with other diagnoses or in people who appear to be well. Sometimes, of course, the positive aspects of studies are emphasized more than they should be and certainly there are examples in the literature of apparent biological correlates of schizophrenia and other psychiatric disorders that appeared convincing and important at one time, but that have not been sustained by subsequent experiments and have faded away 'like elephants' footprints in the mud' (Editorial, *Lancet* 1978). Nevertheless, the more typical picture is of a finding that is made in some experiments and not in others but arises again when tested on further occasions. It is not possible to explain away the positive demonstrations of biological correlates of schizophrenia on the basis of chance, flawed study design, or flawed technique. If then, we have findings of the biological correlates of schizophrenia that are reliably detected in some cases of schizophrenia and not in others then we can only conclude that not all cases of schizophrenia are the same. This biological hetereogeneity has parallels in clinical and phenomenological studies of schizophrenia (Johnstone 1992) and it would be unwise not to consider the possibility that there may be no single key finding, no Holy Grail, and that the causation also may be heterogeneous. Postulation of multi-factorial causation is less intellectually satisfying than the dramatic idea of the discovery of a single cause for the disease. The dream of such a discovery drives many through years of hard work and disappointment but we do our patients no service if we ignore evidence that does not fit in with our chosen ideas. Although the key finding (or findings!) has yet to be made there have been worthwhile advances.

Reasonably successful drug treatments, at least of acute episodes, exist and the mechanism by which they produce their effects is at least partially known. Although I am trained as a clinical scientist, I am aware that my views concerning the basis of schizophrenia are based on faith as well as reason. I certainly believed that schizophrenia was a disorder with a biological basis (which I hoped and still hope to see unravelled in my own lifetime) before it was widely agreed that there was evidence that this was really so. This probably impairs my ability to assess the current state of the evidence in an appropriately objective way but I think it is reasonable to claim that the accumulated burden of evidence from imaging, genetic, neuropathological, neuropsychological, and other biological studies makes it difficult to conclude that this is not a biological disorder even if the nature of this biological disorder is yet unclear. The acceptance that this condition is a disease and that it is thus not a response to imperfect family interactions has certainly brought comfort to some relatives who were understandably extremely distressed by the suggestion that they had driven their children mad, but otherwise our slow and halting progress towards the discovery of the biological basis of schizophrenia has been little help to the sufferers and their carers. Recent clinical studies have demonstrated that the disorder remains common, that in spite of adequate drug treatment, repeated relapse is usual and that for most patients social, occupational, and economic function will be markedly impaired by their illness and the promise that many of them showed in their youth will not be realized. Treatments for acute episodes and for the control of relapse are by no means perfect but they are of undoubted value. The same cannot be said of treatments for negative symptoms where there really is no clear unequivocal evidence of value of any form of drug treatment and where the value of social measures is limited. It is not difficult to argue that it is the slow steady development of the defect state characterized by negative symptoms of apathy, loss of will, inability to respond emotionally, or relate to others, which is the greatest disability suffered by schizophrenic patients. It is often associated with cognitive impairment and, of course, it greatly damages the personality of the sufferer. Not only is there no drug treatment which can be reliably recommended as relieving negative symptoms in the same way that neuroleptics relieve positive symptoms, but we do not really know anything about the determinants of this condition. We do not know whether it continues to progress or if a baseline is really reached after a few years and we do not know what effect cumulative relapses of positive symptoms have upon the defect state.

In the past 30 years the search for the biological basis of schizophrenia has tended to take precedence over studies relating to issues of management. This is understandable. As Kraepelin observed in 1896—as we do not know what causes the illness there cannot be rational treatment—this is true and yet there have been substantial advances in treatment albeit initially serendipitous. Our knowledge of the best way to manage schizophrenia is very limited and perhaps had we appreciated how little practical help for our schizophrenic patients would accrue from the biological studies more applied work might have been carried out. There is more to the management of schizophrenia than drug treatment. There are the fundamental issues of where the patients should live and how much and what kind of support they should have. For 150 years opinion was clear about where mentally ill people should live and that was in mental hospitals, formerly known as asylums. All changed however in the 1960s following the report of Tooth and Brooke (1961), where it was predicted that mental hospitals would be able to be run down and closed and patients discharged into the community. At that time, Mr Enoch Powell was Minister of Health and in a characteristically compelling and vivid speech he said: 'We have to strain to alter our whole mentality about hospitals and about mental hospitals especially. Building hospitals is not like building pyramids—the erection of memorials to endure to a remote posterity. We have to get it into our heads that a hospital is a shell, a framework to contain processes and when the processes change . . . the shell must be scrapped and the framework dismantled'. The situation, of course, was and is that the processes had not changed as much as Mr Powell clearly hoped. The idea of closing the mental hospitals and transferring the patients to the community was developed at a time when there was considerable optimism about the effects of the newly introduced neuroleptic drugs, when it was hoped that the schizophrenic defect state was the result of institutional care rather than a feature of the disorder and when it was 'fashionable' to see the condition as a social response, not an illness.

At that time and indeed since there were scandals relating to mishandling of patients and sadly low standards of care in a number of hospitals. Those of us who have a close acquaintance with a wide range of mental hospitals know that it must have been apparent to the health authorities that more scandals could easily arise and that it would cost a great deal of money to bring the mental hospitals to standards that would be acceptable for acute physical disorders. From the point of view of a government of any political complexion the advantages of the policy of closure of the hospitals and transfer of the patients to community care are obvious—it saved money—it shifted away the responsibility for an area that could go badly wrong at any time, and it seemed progressive. In general, people in diverse professional groups and others who have an interest in this area have either strongly favoured the policy of closure and transfer to community care or have been strongly against it. As is so often the case the strength of their views comes from ideological conviction rather than evidence, because little has been available. Adequate evidence is still lacking but relevant information is beginning to accumulate. The studies described in Chapters 4 and 7 indicate that it is possible for many patients to reside out of hospital although repeated short-lived admissions will be required for many, and, that although problems arise, most patients can be kept in contact with appropriate services and most patients and relatives prefer that the patient continues to live outside of hospital. The planned expansion of community residential facilities appears to have made little impact and the great majority of discharged patients live alone or with relatives. Many appear to think (Johnstone *et al.* 1991*b*) that the services that they receive in terms of hospital or day care, sheltered work, home visits, and outpatient attendances are not adequate or appropriate. Currently, we can express few opinions about this because these forms of management are allocated on the basis of the enthusiasm and resources of local staff and the demands of individual patients. Adequate studies of styles and delivery of care for these patients simply have not been conducted although they are clearly necessary.

It is important that such studies take into account the wishes and views of patients and their carers and indeed these views are important in other areas such as studies of drug treatment. Inadequate attention has perhaps been paid to patients' reasons for non-compliance. The situation, after all, is that reasonably successful drug treatment for acute psychotic episodes and for prophylaxis against relapse is available, but that patients are often unwilling to take it, particularly in a maintenance basis. The work of Hoge *et al.* (1990) shows that while doctors are inclined to take the view that non-compliance results from lack of insight, psychotic reasons, or transference factors, non-compliant patients cite very different reasons, such as side-effects and past experience of lack of efficacy. Consideration of their views may give us earlier information about costs (risks/benefits ratios) of new drugs that may be developed than we have had for those currently in use. Apart from concentrating rather more on management issues than has been customary what should our future research plans be? These can only be described in the broadest of terms. The substantial efforts of many over the last two to three decades have given rise to potential leads at the present time. The principal areas that seem interesting to me may be classed as genetic, pharmacological, imaging, neuropathological, or epidemiological, but for these avenues of exploration to be more fruitful than they have been in the past, the different areas should impact on one another more often than they have tended to do. The familial tendency of schizophrenia at least in some cases is undoubted and it has been shown that this is due to shared genetic material rather than shared environment. Molecular genetic techniques are unlocking the mysteries of other genetic disorders, such as cystic fibrosis and asthma/eczema, but whether these techniques will prove as successful in disorders where the boundaries of the phenotype are unclear, there is no diagnostic test and the onset is at a variable age in adult life is uncertain.

Systematic search of the human genome will be very costly and will take a very long time. The use of candidate genes is clearly a desirable alternative but candidates have to be found. These may come from pharmacological, neuropathological, or even imaging studies. It is fortunate that just as it was becoming clear that study of D_2 receptors was not going to reveal as much about the underlying mechanisms of schizophrenia as was hoped at one time, molecular cloning of subtypes of the dopamine receptor has been successful. It is possible that the effects of 'atypical' anti-psychotic agents upon these receptors may be relevant to their anti-psychotic effect. At present, this is pure speculation. These drugs have a wide range of mechanisms of action and to take the theory that subtypes of dopamine receptor are relevant to schizophrenia any further, drugs which have a relatively pure action upon these subtypes will require to be synthesized and then tested for anti-psychotic effect. Clearly, this will take some time but it is certainly a possible line of research. Various questions which could be answered with structural imaging remain outstanding and, of course, the possibility that functional MRI will prove successful and will allow, in principal, an infinite number of scans in various conditions with the accompliment of neuropsychological testing in one individual is an exciting prospect. With the use of appropriate ligands, SPET and PET imaging allow receptors to be directly studied in life but so far relevant ligands have been few in number. If we accept that the brains of at least some schizophrenic patients are smaller than those of controls then this reduction in size must have a cellular basis and that cellular change cannot be without cause. In spite of all of the difficulties of neuropathological studies in schizophrenia they must be continued but appropriate arrangements for accruing sufficient numbers of well-documented cases are necessary. Embryological studies may be necessary for examining developmental issues and all of this area of work may be appropriately related to genetic studies. Epidemiology is not exciting but it has told us a great deal about the diseases which kill many people in Britain. It would be difficult to see how it could provide information of equal value about a disease which is said to have roughly the same lifetime risk world-wide, but the possibility that viral infection of the mother during pregnancy predisposes to later development of schizophrenia in the child, (referred to in Chapter 8) could be investigated by epidemological means. Although it is my instinctive feeling that the apparent marked increased frequency of schizophrenia in second generation Afro-Caribbean immigrants to Britain will in the end turn out to be explained by diagnostic difficulties, problems in determining the population denominator, and factors relating to substance ingestion, instincts and prejudices are very much the same thing and this possibility, like numerous others, deserves exploration. Research work in schizophrenia is likely to provide employment for many for a long time yet. I wish it were not so.

References

Alexander, P.E., van Kammen, D.P., and Bunney, W.E. (1979). Antispychotic effects of lithium in schizophrenia. *American Journal of Psychiatry*, **136**, 283–7.

Altman, E. and Jobe, T.H. (1992). Phenomenology of psychosis. *Current Opinion in Psychiatry*, **5**, 33–7.

Alzheimer, A. (1897). Beitrage zur pathologischen Anatomie der Hirnrinde und zur anatomischen Grundlage der Psychosen. *Monatsschrift für Psychiatrie und Neurologie*, **2**, 82–120.

Alzheimer, A. (1913). Beitrage zur pathologischen Anatomie der Dementia Praecox. *Allgemeine Zeitschrift für Psychiatrie*, **70**, 810–12.

APA (American Psychiatric Association) (1980). *Diagnostic and statistical manual of mental disorders* (3rd edn). APA, Washington, DC.

APA (American Psychiatric Association) (1987). *Diagnostic and statistical manual of mental disorders* (DSM-III-R) (3rd edn, revised). APA, Washington, DC.

Anderson, C., Connelly, J., Johnstone, E.C., and Owens, D.G.C. (1991). Cause of death, V. In disabilities and circumstances of schizophrenic patients—a follow up study. *British Journal of Psychiatry*, **159** (Suppl. 13), 30–3.

Andreasen, N.C., Olsen, S.A., Dennert, J.W., and Smith, M.R. (1982). Ventricular enlargement in schizophrenia: relationship to positive and negative symptoms. *American Journal of Psychiatry*, **139**, 297–302.

Andreasen, N.C., Swayze, V.W., Flaum, M., Yates, W.R., Arndt, S., and McChesney, C. (1990). Ventricular enlargement in schizophrenia. Evaluated with computed tomographic scanning: effects of gender, age and stage of illness. *Archives of General Psychiatry*, **47**, 1008–15.

Angrist, B., Sathanathan, G., Wilk, S., and Gershon, S. (1974). Amphetamine psychosis: behavioural and biochemical aspects. *Journal of Psychiatric Research*, **11**, 13–23.

Angrist, B., Rotrosen, J., and Gershon, S. (1980). Differential effects of amphetamine and neuroleptics on negative vs. positive symptoms in schizophrenia. *Psychopharmacology*, **72**, 17–19.

Aretaeus, the Cappadocian (AD 200). *The extant works* (trans. Francis Adams, 1856). Facsimile edition (1972). Milford House, Boston, Mass.

Asano, N. (1967). Pneumoencephalographic study of schizophrenia. In *Clinical genetics in psychiatry* (ed. H. Mitsuda), pp. 209–19. Igaku Shain, Tokyo.

Astrachan, B.M., Harrow, M., Adler, D., Braner, L., Schwartz, C., and Tucker, G. (1972). A check list for the diagnosis of schizophrenia. *British Journal of Psychiatry*, **121**, 529–39.

Barton, R. (1959). *Institutional neurosis*. John Wright, Bristol.

Bateson, G., Jackson, D.D., Haley, J., and Weakland, J.H. (1956). Towards a theory of schizophrenia. *Behavioural Science*, **1**, 251.

Bech, P., Rafaelsen, O.J., Kramp, P., and Bolwig, T. (1978). The mania rating scale; scale construction and inter-observer agreement. *Neuropharmacology*, **17**, 430–1.

Belliveau, J.W. *et al.* (1991). Functional mapping of the human visual cortex by magnetic resonance imaging. *Science*, **254**, 716–19.

Ben-Jonathan, N., Oliver, C., Weiner, H.J., Mical, R.S., and Porter, J.C. (1977). Dopamine in hypophyseal portal plasma of the rat during the oestrous cycle and throughout pregnancy. *Endocrinology*, **100**, 452–8.

Bench, C.J., Dolan, R.J., Friston, K.J., and Frackowiak, R.S.J. (1990). Position emission tomography in the study of brain metabolism in psychiatric and neuropsychiatric disorders. *British Journal of Psychiatry*, **157** (suppl. 9), 82–95.

Bennett, J.P. and Snyder, S.H. (1975). Stereospecific binding of D-lysergic acid diethylamide (LSD) to brain membranes: relationship to serotonin receptors. *Brain Research*, **94**, 523.

Berson, S.A. and Yalow, R.S. (1968). General principles of radio immuno assay. *Clinical Chemistry Acta*, **22**, 51–69.

Biederman, J., Lerner, Y., and Belmaker, R.H. (1979). Combination of lithium carbonate and haloperidol in schizo-affective disorder. *Archives of General Psychiatry*, **36**, 327–33.

Bird, E.D., Spokes, E.G., Barnes, J., Mackay, A.V.P., Iversen, L.L., and Shepherd, M. (1977). Increased brain dopamine and reduced glutamic acid decarboxylase and choline acetyl transferase in schizophrenia and related psychoses. *Lancet*, **ii**, 1157–9.

Bird, E.D. *et al.* (1979). Dopamine and homovanillic acid concentrations in the post mortem brain in schizophrenia. *Journal of Physiology*, **293**, 36–7.

Bishop, M.P., Gallant, D.M., and Sykes, T.F. (1965). Extrapyramidal side effects and therapeutic response. *Archives of General Psychiatry*, **13**, 155–62.

Blair, J.H., Smiffen, R.C., Cranswick, E.H., Jaffe, W., and Kline, N.S. (1952). The question of histopathological changes in the testes of schizophrenia. *Journal of Mental Science*, **98**, 464–5.

Bleuler, E. (1911/1950). *Dementia praecox or the group of schizophrenias* (trans. Joseph Zinkin). International Universities Press, New York.

Bleuler, M. (1978). *The schizophrenic disorders* (trans. M. Clemens). Yale University Press, New Haven, Conn.

Bogerts, B., Meerts, E., and Schonfeldt-Bausch, R. (1985). Basal ganglia and limbic system pathology in schizophrenia; a morphometric study of brain volume and shrinkage. *Archives of General Psychiatry*, **42**, 784–91.

Borenstein, P., Dabbah, M., and Metzger, J. (1957). L'encephalographie fractionée dans les syndromes schizophreniques. *Annales Medico- Psychologiques.*, **155**, 386–425.

Bourdillon, R.E., Clarke, C.A., Ridges, AP., Sheppard, P.M., Harper, P., and Leslie, S.A. (1965). 'Pink spot' in the urine of schizophrenics. *Nature (London)*, **208**, 453.

Bowers, M.B. (1974). Central dopamine turnover in schizophrenic syndromes. *Archives of General Psychiatry*, **31**, 50–4.

Bowler, A.E. and Torrey, E.F. (1990). Influenza and schizophrenia. *Archives of General Psychiatry*, **46**, 878–82.

Brockington, I.F. and Leff, J.P. (1979). Schizo affective psychosis definitions and incidence. *Psychological Medicine*, **9**, 91–9.

Brockington, I.F., Kendell, R.E., and Wainwright, S. (1980). Depressed patients with schizophrenic or paranoid symptoms. *Psychological Medicine*, **10**, 665–75.

Brown, G.W. and Birley, J.L.T. (1968). Crises and life changes and the onset of schizophrenia. *Journal of Health and Human Behaviour*, **9**, 203–14.

Brown, G.W., Birley, J.L.T., and Wing, J.K. (1972). Influence of family life on the course of schizophrenia. *British Journal of Psychiatry*, **121**, 241–58.

Brown, R. *et al.* (1986). Postmortem evidence of structural brain changes in schizophrenia; differences in brain weight, temporal horn area and parahippocampal gyrus compared with affective disorder. *Archives of General Psychiatry*, **43**, 36–42.

Bruton, C.J., Crow, T.J., Frith, C.D., Johnstone, E.C., Owens, D.G.C., and Roberts, G.W. (1990). Schizophrenia and the brain; a prospective clinico neuropathological study. *Psychological Medicine*, **20**, 285–304.

Burt, D.R., Creese, I., and Snyder, S.H. (1977). Antischizophrenic drugs: chronic treatment elevates dopamine receptor binding in the brain. *Science*, **196**, 326–8.

Cancro, R. (1983). Towards a unified view of schizophrenic disorders. In *Affective and schizophrenic disorders* (ed. M Zates). Brunner Mazel, New York.

Carlsson, A. and Lindqvist, M. (1963). Effect of chlorpromazine and halopendol on formation of 3-methoxy-tyramine and normetanephrine in mouse brain. *Acta Pharmacologica et Toxicologica*, **20**, 140–4.

Carpenter, W.T., Strauss, J.S., and Bartko, J.J. (1973). Flexible system for the diagnosis of schizophrenia; report from the WIIO International Pilot Study of Schizophrenia. *Science*, **182**, 1275–8.

Castelao, J.F., Ferreira, L., Geldeis, Y.G., and Heylen, S.L.E. (1989). The efficacy of the D2 and 5HT2 antagonist risperidone (R64766) in the treatment of chronic psychosis. An open dose finding study. *Schizophrenia Research*, **2**, 411–15.

Castle, D.J. and Murray, R.M. (1991). The neurodevelopmental basis of sex differences in schizophrenia. *Psychological Medicine*, **21**, 565–76.

Cheadle, A.J., Freeman, H.L., and Korer, J.R. (1978). Chronic schizophrenic patients in the community. *British Journal of Psychiatry*, **132**, 221–7.

Ciompi, L. (1980). The natural history of schizophrenia in the long term. *British Journal of Psychiatry*, **136**, 413–20.

Clement-Cormier, Y.C., Kebabian, J.W., Petzold, G.L., and Greengard, P. (1974). Dopamine sensitive adenylate cyclase in mammalian brain: a possible site of action of antipsychotic drugs. *Proceedings of the National Academy of Sciences, USA*, **71**, 1113–17.

Clouston, T.S. (1890). *Clinical Lectures on mental diseases*, (6th edn) Churchill, London.

Clouston, T.S. (1891). *The neuroses of development being the Morison Lectures of 1890*. Oliver & Boyd, Edinburgh.

Cole, J.O. and Clyde D. (1961). Extrapyramidal side effects and clinical response to the phenothiazines. *Rev. Can. Biol.*, **20**, 565–74.

Connell, P.H. (1958). Amphetamine psychosis. *Maudsley Monograph*, No 5. Chapman & Hall, London.

Cooper, J.E., Kendell, R.E., Gurland, B.J. Sharpe, L., Copeland, J.R.M., and Simon, R. (1972). Psychiatric diagnosis in New York and London. *Maudsley Monograph*, No. 20. Oxford University Press.

Cotes, P.M., Crow, T.J., Johnstone, E.C., Bartlett, W., and Bourne, R.C. (1978). Neuroendocrine changes in acute schizophrenia as a function of clinical state and neuroleptic medication. *Psychological Medicine*, **8**, 657–65.

Crane, G.E. and Paulson, G. (1966). Involuntary movements in a sample of chronic mental patients and their relation to the treatment with neuroleptics. *International Journal of Neuropsychiatry*, **3**, 286–91.

Crawley, J.C.W., *et al.* (1986). Uptake of 77Br-Spiperone in the striata of schizophrenic patients. *Nuclear Medicine Communications*, **7**, 599–706.

Creer, C. (1975). Living with schizophrenia. *Social Work Today*, **6**, 2–7.

Creer, C. and Wing, J.K. (1974). *Schizophrenia at home*. National Schizophrenia Fellowship, 79 Victoria Road, Surbiton, Surrey, KT6 4JF.

Creese, I., Burt, D.R., and Snyder, S.H. (1976). Dopamine receptor binding predicts clinical and pharmacological potencies of antischizophrenic drugs. *Science*, **192**, 481–3.

Creese, I., Burt, D.R., and Snyder, S.H. (1978). Biochemical actions of neuroleptic drugs: focus on the dopamine receptor. In *Handbook of psychopharmacology*, (ed. L.L. Iversen, S.D. Iversen, and S.H. Snyder), Vol. 10, pp. 37–89. Plenum, New York.

Crow, T.J. (1980). Molecular pathology of schizophrenia; more than one disease process. *British Medical Journal*, **280**, 66–8.

Crow, T.J. (1986). The continuum of psychosis and its implications for the structure of the gene. *British Journal of Psychiatry*, **149**, 419–29.

Crow, T.J. and Mitchell, W.S. (1975). Subjective age in chronic schizophrenia: evidence for a subgroup of patients with defective learning capacity. *British Journal of Psychiatry*, **126**, 360–3.

Crow, T.J. *et al.* (1979*a*). Monoamine mechanisms in chronic schizophrenia: post mortem neurochemical findings. *British Journal of Psychiatry*, **134**, 249–56.

Crow, T.J., Johnstone, E.C., and Owen, F. (1979*b*). Research on schizophrenia. In *Recent advances in clinical psychiatry* (ed. K Granville-Grossman). Churchill-Livingstone, London.

Crow, T.J., Cross, A.J., Johnstone, E.C., and Owen, F. (1982). Two syndromes in schizophrenia and their pathogenesis. In *Schizophrenia as a brain disease* (ed. F.A. Henn and H.A. Nasrallah), pp. 196–234. Oxford University Press.

Crow, T.J., Macmillan, J.F., Johnson, A.L., and Johnstone, E.C. (1986). The Northwick Park study of first episodes of schizophrenia. II:A randomised controlled trial of prophylactic neuroleptic treatment. *British Journal of Psychiatry*, **148**, 120–7.

Crow, T.J., Colter, N., Brown, R., Bruton, C.J., and Johnstone, E.C. (1988). Lateralised asymmetry of temporal horn enlargement in schizophrenia. *Schizophrenia Research*, **I**, 155–6.

Crow, T.J., Done, D.J., and Johnstone, E.C. (1991*a*). Schizophrenia and Influenza. *Lancet*, **338**, 116–17.

Crow, T.J., Done, D.J., Johnstone, E.C., and Sacker, A. (1991*b*). *Childhood precursors of adult psychosis*. Presented at American College of Neuropsyohopharmacology, Puerto Rico.

Curson, D.A., Pantelis, C., Ward, J., and Barnes, T.R.E. (1992). Institutionalism and schizophrenia 30 years on. *British Journal of Psychiatry*, **160**, 230–41.

Dalen, P. (1975). *Season of birth: a study of schizophrenia and other mental disorders*. North-Holland Elsevier. New York.

Dandy, W.E. (1919). Roentgenography of the brain after injection of air into the cerebral ventricles. *American Journal of Roentgenography*, **6**, 26.

David, G.B. (1957). The pathological anatomy of the schizophrenias. In *Schizophrenia, somatic aspects* (ed. D Richter), pp. 93–130. Pergamon, New York.

Davis, J. (1975). Overview: maintenance therapy in psychiatry and schizophrenia. *American Journal of Psychiatry*, **132**, 1237–45.

Davison, K. (1983). Schizophrenia-like psychoses associated with organic cerebral disorders: a review. *Psychiatric Developments*, **i**, 1–34.

Davison, K. and Bagley, C.R. (1969). Schizophrenia-like psychoses associated with organic disorders of the nervous system: a review of the literature. In *Current problems in neuropsychiatry* (ed. R N Herrington). Headley Brothers, Ashford, Kent.

De Lisi, L. (1992). Recent advances in the genetics of schizophrenia. In *New biological vistas on schizophrenia* (ed. J.P. Lindenmayer and S.R. Kay). Brunner Mazel, New York.

Deakin, J.F.W., Slater, P., and Simpson, M. (1989). Frontal cortical and left temporal glutamatergic dysfunction in schizophrenia. *Journal of Neurochemistry*, **52**, 1781–6.

Delay, J. and Deniker, P. (1952). Le traitment des psychoses par une méthode neurolytique derivée de l'hibernothérapie. In *Congrés de Médicines Aliénistes et Neurologistes de France* (ed. P Cossa), pp. 497–502. Masson Editeurs Libraires de L'Academie de Médicine, Paris & Luxembourg.

Delva, N.J. and Letemendia, F. (1982). Lithium treatment in schizophrenia and schizo affective disorders. *British Journal of Psychiatry*, **141**, 387–400.

Deniker, P. (1960). Experimental neurological synchromes and the new drug therapics in psychiatry. *Comprehensive Psychiatry*, **1**, 92–102.

Donaldson, S.R., Gelenberg, A.T., and Baldessarini, R.J. (1983). The pharmacologic treatment of schizophrenia: a progress report. *Schizophrenia Bulletin*, **9**, 504–27.

Done, D.J., Johnstone, E.C., Frith, C.D., Golding, J., Shepherd, P.M., and Crow T.J. (1991). Complications of pregnancy and delivery in relation to psychosis in adult life. Data from the British perinatal mortality survey sample. *British Medical Journal*, **302**, 1576–80.

Drake, R.E. and Cotton, P.G. (1986). Depression, hopelessness and suicide in chronic schizophrenia. *British Journal of Psychiatry*, **148**, 554–9.

Dulz, B. and Hand, I. (1986). Short-term relapse in young schizophrenics. Can it be predicted and affected by family (CFI) patient and treatment variables? In *Treatment of schizophrenia* (ed. M. J. Goldstein, I. Hand, and K. Haplweg), pp. 59–75, Springer, Berlin.

Dunlap, C.B. (1924). Dementia praecox: some preliminary observations on brains from carefully selected cases and a consideration of certain sources of error. *American Journal of Psychiatry*, **80**, 403–21.

Eagles, J.M., Gibson, I., Bremner, M.H., Clunie, F., and Ebmeier, K.P. (1990). Obstetric complications in DSM III schizophrenics and their siblings. *Lancet*, **ii**, 1139–41.

Egeland, J.R. *et al.* (1987). Bipolar affective disorders linked to DNA markers in chromosome, II. *Nature*, **325**, 783–7.

Enna, S.J., Bennett, J.P., Burt, D.R., Creese, I., and Snyder, S.H. (1976). Stereospecificity of interaction of neuroleptic drugs with neurotransmitters and correlation with clinical potency. *Nature (London)*, **263**, 338–41.

Falconer, D.S. (1965). The inheritance of liability to certain diseases estimated from the incidence among relatives. *Annals of Human Genetics*, **29**, 51–76.

Farde, L, Wiesel, F.A., and Hall, H. (1987). No D-2 receptor increase in PET study of schizophrenia. *Archives of General Psychiatry*, **44**, 671.

Farde, L., Wiesel, F.A., Halldin, C., Stone-Elander, S., and Nordstrom, A.L. (1990). D2 Dopamine receptor characteristics in neuroleptic-naive patients with schizophrenia. *Archives of General Psychiatry*, **47**, 213–19.

Feighner, J.P., Robins, E., Guze, S., Woodruff, R.A., Winokur, G., and Munoz, R. (1972). Diagnostic criteria for use in psychiatric research. *Archives of General Psychiatry*, **26**, 57–62.

Ferrier, I.N., Johnstone, E.C., Crow, T.J., and Rincon-Rodriguez, I. (1983). Anterior pituitary hormone secretion in chronic schizophrenia. *Archives of General Psychiatry*, **40**, 755–61.

Fink, P.J. and Weinstein, S.P. (1979). Whatever happened to psychiatry? The deprofessionalisation of community mental health centers. *American Journal of Psychiatry*, **136**, 406–9.

Fischer-Cornelssen, K.A. and Ferner, U.J. (1976). An example of European multicenter trials: multispectral analysis of clozapine. *Psychopharmacology Bulletin*, **12**, 34–9.

Flugel, F. (1953). Thérapeutique par médication neuroleptique obtenue en réalisant systematiquement des états Parkinsoniformes. *L'Encéphale*, **45**, 1090–2.

FDA (Food and Drug Administration) Task Force, American College of Neuropsychopharmacology (1973). Neurological syndromes associated with antipsychotic drug use. *New England Journal of Medicine*, **289**, 20–3.

Friedberg, J. (1977). Shock treatment brain damage and memory loss: a neurological perspective. *American Journal of Psychiatry*. **134**, 1010–4.

Friedhoff, A.J. and Van Winkle, E. (1962). Isolation and characterisation of the compound from the urine of schizophrenics. *Nature*, **194**, 897.

Frith, C.D. (1977). Two kinds of cognitive deficit associated with chronic schizophrenia. *Psychological Medicine*, **7**, 171–3.

Frith, C.D. (1987). The positive and negative symptoms of schizophrenia reflect impairments in the perception and initiation of action. *Psychological Medicine*, **17**, 631–48.

Frith, C.D. (1992). *The cognitive neuropsychology of schizophrenia*. Lawrence Erlbaum Associatea, Hove

Frith, C.D., Leary, J., Cahill, C., and Johnstone, E.C. (1991). Performance on psychological tests, IV. In disabilities and circumstances of schizophrenic patients—A follow up study. *British Journal of Psychiatry*, **159**, (suppl. 13), 26–9.

Furlong, R. (1987). The care of the very sick—the role of the institution. In *Schizophrenia* (ed. Katia G. Herbst), pp. 57–62, Mental Health Foundation, London.

Fuxe, K. and Hokfelt. (1969). Catecholamines in the hypothalamus and the pituitary gland. In *Frontiers in neuroendocrinology*, (ed. W.F. Ganong and L. Martini). Oxford University Press.

Fromm-Reichman, F. (1948). Notes on the development of treatment of schizophrenics by psychoanalytic psychotherapy. *Psychiatry*, **11**, 263–73.

Garmezy, N. (1978). Attentional processes in adult schizophrenia and children at risk. *Journal of Psychiatric Research*, **14**, 3–34.

Gattaz, W.F., Gattaz, D., and Beckmann, H. (1982). Glutamate in schizophrenics and healthy controls. *Archiv für Psychiatrie und Nervenkrank Leiten*, **231**, 221–5.

Gattaz, W.F., Kohlmeyer, K., and Gasser, T. (1991). Computer tomographic studies in Schizophrenia. In *Search for the causes of schizophrenia* (ed. H. Hafner and W.F. Gattaz), pp. 242–56, Springer, Berlin.

Gawler, J., Bull, J.W.D., Du Boulay, G.H., and Marshall, J. (1975). Computerized axial tomography: the normal EMI scan. *Journal of Neurology Neurosurgery and Psychiatry*, **38**, 935–47.

Gelders, Y., Heylen, S., Vanden Busche, G., Reyntjens, A, and Janssen, P. (1990). Serotonin 5HT2 receptor antagonism in the treatment of schizophrenia. *Clinical Neuropharmacology*, **13**, 182–3.

Gjessing, R. (1938). Disturbances of somatic functions in catatonia with a period course and their compensation. *Journal of Mental Science*, **84**, 608–21.

Goldberg, E.M. and Morrison, S.L. (1963). Schizophrenia and social class. *British Journal of Psychiatry*, **109**, 785–802.

Goldberg, S.C., Klerman, G.L., and Cole, J.O. (1965). Changes in schizophrenic psychopathology and ward behaviour as a function of phenothiazine treatment. *British Journal of Psychiatry*, **111**, 120–33.

Griffith R.W. and Saameli, K. (1975). Clozapine and agranulocytosis. *Lancet*, **2**, 657.

Griffiths, J.D., Cavanaugh, J., Held, J., and Oates, J.A. (1972). Dextramphetamine: evaluation of psychomimetic properties in man. *Archives of General Psychiatry*, **26**, 97–100.

Haase, H. (1962). Intensity and equivalence of neuroleptic effect and its therapeutic importance. *Nervenarzt*, **33**, 213–20.

Hafner, H., Haas, S., Ffeifer-Kurda, M., Eichborn, S., and Michitsuji, S. (1987). Abnormal seasonality of schizophrenic births: a specific finding? *European Archives of Psychiatry and Neurological Science*, **236**, 333–42.

Hafner, H., Riecher, A., and Maurer, K. (1989). How does gender influence age at first hospitalisation for schizophrenia? A transnational case register study. *Psychological Medicine*, **19**, 903–18.

Hall, J.N. (1980). Ward rating scales for long-stay patients: a review. *Psychological Medicine*, **10**, 277–88.

Hammond, T. (1987). When they are not in hospital, where should they be? In *Schizophrenia* (ed. K.G. Herbst). Mental Health Foundation, London.

Harding, C.M., Brooks, G.W., Ashikaga, T., Strauss, J.S., and Breier, A. (1987). The Vermont longitudinal study of persons with severe mental illness. I: methodology, study sample and overall status 32 years later. *American Journal of Psychiatry*, **144**, 718–26.

Hare, E.H. and Walter, S.D. (1978). Seasonal variation in admissions of psychiatric patients and its relation to seasonal variation in their births. *Journal of Epidemiology and Community Health*, **32**, 47–52.

Harris, A. and Norris, V. (1955). Expectation of life and liberty in patients suffering from functional psychoses. *Psychiatric Quarterly*, **29**, 33–47.

Harrison, G., Owens, D., Holton, A., Neilson, D., and Boot, D. (1988). A prospective study of severe mental disorder in Afro Caribbean patients. *Psychological Medicine*, **18**, 643–57.

Harrison, G., Holton, A., Neilson, D., Owens, D., Boot, D., and Cooper, J. (1989). Severe mental disorder in Afro Caribbean patients: some social demographic and service factors. *Psychological Medicine*, **19**, 683–96.

Harvey, I. and Murray, R.M. (1990). Why Kraepelin was wrong: the neurodevelopmental view of dementia praecox. In *Psychiatry: A world perspective*, Vol. I (ed. C.N. Stefanis *et al.*), Elsevier, Amsterdam.

Haslam, J. (1809). *Observations on madness and melancholy*, Rivington, London.

Haug, J.O. (1962). Pneumoencephalographic studies in mental disease. *Acta Psychiatrica Scandinavica*, **38**, (Suppl. 165), 1–104.

Haug, J.O. (1982). Pneumencephalographic evidence of brain atrophy in acute and chronic schizophrenic patients. *Acta Psychiatrica Scandinavica*, **66**, 374–83.

Hecker, E. (1871). Die Hebephrenie. Ein Beitrag zur klinischen Psychiatrie. *Archiv für pathologische Anatomie und Physiologie und für klinische Medizin*, **52**, 394–429.

Hemphill, R.E., Reiss, M., and Taylor, A.L. (1944). A study of the histology of the testis in schizophrenia and other mental disorders. *Journal of Mental Science*, **90**, 681–95.

Hemsley, D.R. (1982). Cognitive impairment in schizophrenia. In *The pathology and psychology of cognition* (ed. A Burton), pp. 169–203. Methuen, London.

Hirsch, S.R., Gaind, R., Rohde, P.D., Stevens, B.C., and Wing, J.K. (1973). Outpatient maintenance of chronic schizophrenic patients with long acting fluphenazine double blind placebo controlled trial. *British Medical Journal*, **1**, 633–7.

Hirsch, S. and Leff, J.P. (1975). Abnormalities in parents of schizophrenics. *Maudsley Monograph*, No. 22. Oxford University Press.

Hirschowitz, J., Caspar, R., Garver, D.L., and Chang, S. (1980). Lithium response in good prognosis schizophrenia. *American Journal of Psychiatry*, **137**, 916–20.

HMSO (1980). *Classification of occupations of the Register General* Her Majesty's Staionary Office, London.

Hogarty, G.E., and Goldberg, S.C. (1977). Temporal effects of drugs and placebo in delaying relapse in schizophrenic outpatients. *Archives of General Psychiatry*, **34**, 297–301.

Hogarty, G.E., Goldberg, S.C., and the Collaborative Study Group. (1973). Drugs and socio-therapy in the aftercare of schizophrenic patients, one year relapse rates. *Archives of General Psychiatry*, **28**, 54–64.

Hogarty, G.E., Goldberg, S.C., Schooler, N.R., and Ulrich, R.F. (1974). Collaborative Study Group: Drugs and socio-therapy in the aftercare of schizophrenic patients. II: two year relapse rates. *Archives of General Psychiatry*, **31**, 603–8.

Hogarty, G.E., Schooler, N.R., Ulrich, R.F., Mussare, F., Ferro, P, and Nerron, E. (1979). Fluphenazine and social therapy in the aftercare of schizophrenic patients. *Archives of General Psychiatry*, **36**, 1283–94.

Hogarty, G.E. *et al.* (1988). dose of fluphenazine decanoate, familial expressed emotion and outcome in schizophrenia. Results of a two year controlled study. *Archives of General Psychiatry*, **45**, 797–805.

Hoge, S.K. *et al.* (1990). A prospective multicenter study of patients refusal of antipsychotic medication. *Archives of General Psychiatry*, **47**, 949–56.

Hollister, L.E. and Friedhoff, A.J. (1966). Effects of 3:4 dimethoxyphenylethylamine in man. *Nature (London)*, **210**, 1377.

Hornykiewicz, O. (1973). Dopamine in the basal ganglia; its role and therapeutic implications. *British Medical Bulletin*, **29**, 172–8.

Hounsfield, G.N. (1973). Computerised transverse axial scanning (tomography). Part I: Description of the system. *British Journal of Radiology*, **46**, 1016–22.

Huber, G. (1957). *Pneumoencephalographische und Psychopathologische Bilder Bei Endogen Psychosen*. Springer-Verlag, Berlin.

Hunter, R., Jones, M., and Cooper, F. (1968). Modified lumbar air ence-phalography in the investigation of long stay psychiatric patients. *Journal of Neurological Science*, **6**, 597–600.

Illowsky, B.P., Juliano, D.M., Bigelaw, L.B., and Weinberger, D.R. (1988). Stability of CT scan findings in schizophrenia: results of an eight year follow up study. *Journal of Neurology, Neurosurgery and Psychiatry*, **51**, 209–13.

Ingvar, D.H. (1987). Evidence for frontal/prefrontal cortical dysfunction in chronic schizophrenia: the phenomenon of hypofrontality reconsidered. In *Biological Perspectives of Schizophrenia* (ed. 4. Helmchen and F.A. Henn), pp. 201–41. John Wiley and S. Bernhardt. Dahlem Konferenzen 1987, Chichester.

Iversen, L.L. (1975). Dopamine receptors in the brain. *Science*, **188**, 1084–9.

Jacobi, W. and Winkler, H. (1927). Encephalographische Studien an chronisch Schizophrenen. *Archiv für Psychiatrik Nervenkrank*, **81**, 299–332.

Jakob, H. and Beckmann, H. (1986). Prenatal development disturbances in the limbic allocortex in schizophrenics. *Journal of Neural Transmission*, **65**, 303–26.

Javitt, D.C. and Zukin, S.R. (1990). Role of excitatory amino acids in neuro-psychiatric illness. *Journal of Neuropsychiatry and Clinical Neuroscience*, **2**, 44–52.

Jellinger, K. (1985). Neuromorphological background of pathochemical studies in major psychoses. In *Pathochemical markers in major psychoses* (ed. H. Beckmann and P. Riederer), pp. 1–23, Springer, Heidelberg.

Jernigan, T.L., Zatz, L.M., Moses, J.A., and Berger, P.A. (1982). Computed tomography in schizophrenics and normal volunteers. *Archives of General Psychiatry*, **39**, 765–70.

Johnstone, E.C. (1978). The clinical implications of dopamine receptor blockade in acute schizophrenia. In *Neuroleptics and schizophrenia*, (ed. J.M. Simister). Lundbeck, Letchworth.

Johnstone, E.C. (1987). Physical treatments. *British Medical Bulletin*, **43**, 689–703.

Johnstone, E.C. (1991). New developments in antipsychotic drug therapy. In *Current practices and future developments in the pharmacotherapy of mental disorders* (ed. H. Meltzer and D. Nerozzi). Excerpta Medica, Amsterdam.

Johnstone, E.C. (1992). Heterogeneity in schizophrenia. Clinical and biological aspects. *New biological vistas on schizophrenia* (ed. J.P. Lindermayer and S.R. Kay). Brunner Mazel, New York.

Johnstone, E.C., Crow, T.J., Frith, C.D., Husband, J., and Kreel, L. (1976). Cerebral ventricular size and cognitive impairment in chronic schizophrenia. *Lancet*, **ii**, 924–6.

Johnstone, E.C., Crow, T.J., Frith, C.D., Stevens, M., Kreel, L., and Husband, J. (1978a). The dementia of dementia praecox. *Acta Psychiatrica Scandinavica*, **57**, 305–24.

Johnstone, E.C., Crow, T.J., Frith, C.D., Carney, M.W.P., and Price, J.S. (1978b). Mechanism of the antipsychotic effect in the treatment of acute schizophrenia. *Lancet*, **i**, 848–51.

Johnstone, E.C., Owens, D.G.C., Gold, A., Crow, T.J., and Macmillan, J.F. (1981). Institutionalisation and the defects of schizophrenia. *British Journal of Psychiatry*, **139**, 195–203.

Johnstone, E.C. *et al.* (1983). Adverse effects of anticholinergic medication on positive schizophrenic symptoms. *Psychological Medicine*, **13**, 513–27.

Johnstone, E.C., Owens, D.G.C., Gold, A., Crow, T.J., and Macmillan, J.F. (1984). Schizophrenic patients discharged from hospital. *British Journal of Psychiatry*, **145**, 586–90.

Johnstone, E.C., Owens, D.G.C., Frith, C.D., and Calvert, L.M. (1985). Institutionalisation and the outcome of functional psychoses. *British Journal of Psychiatry*, **146**, 36–44.

Johnstone, E.C., Crow, T.J., Macmillan, J.F., Owens, D.G.C., Bydder, G.M., and Steiner, R.E. (1986a). A magnetic resonance study of early schizophrenia. A controlled magnetic resonance imaging study. *Journal of Neurology, Neurosurgery and Psychiatry*, **49**, 136–9.

Johnstone, E.C., Crow, T.J., Johnson, A.L., and Macmillan, J.F. (1986b). The Northwick Park study of first episodes of schizophrenia. I: Presentation of the illness and problems relating to admission. *British Journal of Psychiatry*, **148**, 115–20.

Johnstone, E.C., Owens, D.G.C. Frith, C.D., and Crow, T.J. (1987a). The relative stability of positive and negative features in chronic schizophrenia. *British Journal of Psychiatry*, **150**, 60–4.

Johnstone, E.C., Macmillan, J.F., and Crow, T.J. (1987b). The occurrence of organic disease of possible or probably aetiological significance in a population of 268 cases of first episode schizophrenia. *Psychological Medicine*, **17**, 371–9.

Johnstone, E.C., Crow, T.J., Frith, C.D., and Owens, D.G.C. (1988a). The Northwick Park 'functional' psychoses study: diagnosis and treatment response. *Lancet*, **ii**, 119–26.

Johnstone, E.C., Cooling, N., Frith, C.D., Crow, T.J., and Owens, D.G.C. (1988b). Phenomenology of organic and functional psychoses and the overlap between them. *British Journal of Psychiatry*, **153**, 770–6.

Johnstone, E.C. *et al.* (1989a). The spectrum of structural brain changes in schizophrenia: age of onset as a predictor of cognitive and clinical impairments and their cerebral correlates. *Psychological Medicine*, **19**, 91–103.

Johnstone, E.C. *et al.* (1989b). Temporal lobe structure as determined by nuclear magnetic resonance in schizophrenia and bipolar affective disorder. *Journal of Neurology, Neurosurgery and Psychiatry*, **52**, 736–41.

Johnstone, E.C., Macmillan, J.F., Frith, C.D., Benn, D.K., and Crow, T.J. (1990). Further investigation of the predictors of outcome following first schizophrenic episodes. *British Journal of Psychiatry*, **157**, 182–9.

Johnstone, E.C., Crow, T.J., Owens, D.G.C., and Frith, C.D. (1991a). The Northwick Park 'functional' psychosis study. Phase 2: Maintenance treatment. *Journal of Psychopharmacology*, **5**, 388–95.

Johnstone, E.C. *et al.* (1991b). Disabilities and circumstances of schizophrenic patients—a follow up study. *British Journal of Psychiatry*, **159**, (Suppl. 13.).

Johnstone, E.C. *et al.* (1992). The Northwick Park 'functional' psychosis study: diagnosis and outcome. *Psychological Medicine*, **22**, 331–46.

Johnstone, E.C., Bruton, C.J., Crow, T.J., Frith, C.D., and Owens, D.G.C. (in press.). Clinical correlates of post mortem brain changes in schizophrenia. *Journal of Neurology, Neurosurgery and Psychiatry*.

Jones, K. (1987). Why a crisis situation? What has happened? In *Schizophrenia* (ed. K Herbst), pp. 47–52. Mental Health Foundation, London.

Jones, K. and Poletti, A. (1985). Understanding the Italian experience. *British Journal of Psychiatry*, **146**, 341–7.

Jones, K. and Poletti, A. (1986). The Italian experience reconsidered. *British Journal of Psychiatry*, **148**, 144–50.

Kahlbaum, K.L. (1874). Die Katatonie order das Spannungirresein. *Eine klinische Form psychischer Krankheit*. Hirschwald, Berlin.

Kane, J.M. and Rifkin, A. (1985). High dose vs. low dose strategies in the treatment of schizophrenia. *Psychopharmacology Bulletin*, **21**, 533.

Kane, J.M., and Rifkin, A., Quitkin, F., Nayak, D., and Ramos Lorenzi, J. (1982). Fluphenazine vs. placebo in patients with remitted acute first episode schizophrenia. *Archives of General Psychiatry*, **39**, 70–3.

Kane, J., Honigfeld, G., Singer, J., and Meltzer, H. (1988) Clozapine for the treatment resistant schizophrenic: a double blind comparison versus chlorpromazine/benztropine. *Archives of General Psychiatry*, **45**, 789–96.

Karno, M. *et al.* (1987). Expressed emotion and schizophrenia outcome among Mexican-American families. *Journal of Neurosis and Mental Disease*, **175**, 143–51.

Kasanin, J. (1933). The acute schizo affective psychoses. *American Journal of Psychiatry*, **90**, 97–126.

Kaufmann, C.A., De Lisi, L.E., Bassett, A.S., Gershon, E.S., and Gilliam, T.C. (1989). Physical mapping and linkage analysis of a susceptibility locus for schizophrenia on chromosome 5g. *Schizophrenia Bulletin*, **15**, 441–52.

Kebabian, J.W., Petzold, G.L., and Greengard, P. (1972). Dopamine sensitive adenylate cyclase in candate nucleus of rat brain and its similarity to the 'dopamine receptor'. *Proceedings of the National Academy of Sciences (USA)*, **69**, 2145–9.

Kelsoe, J.R. *et al.* (1989). Re-evaluation of the linkage relationship between chromosome 11p locus and the gene for affective disorder in the Old Order Amish. *Nature*, **342**, 238–43.

Kendell, R.E. (1986). The classification and phenomenology of schizophrenia. In *Contemporary issues in schizophrenia* (ed. A. Kerr and P. Snaith). Gaskell, Royal College of Psychiatrists, London.

Kendell, R.E. and Brockington, I.F. (1980). The identification of disease entities and the relationship between schizophrenia and affective psychoses. *British Journal of Psychiatry*, **137**, 324–31.

Kendell, R.E. and Gourlay, J. (1970). The clinical distinction between the affective psychoses and schizophrenia. *British Journal of Psychiatry*, **117**, 261–6.

Kendell, R.E. and Kemp, I.W. (1989). Maternal influenza in the aetiology of schizophrenia. *Archives of General Psychiatry*, **46**, 878–82.

Kendell, R.E., Brockington, I.F., and Leff, J.P. (1979). Prognostic implications of six alternative definitions of schizophrenia. *Archives of General Psychiatry*, **35**, 25–31.

Kendler, K.S. (1987). The feasibility of linkage studies in schizophrenia. In *Biological perspectives of schizophrenia* (ed. H. Helmchen and F.A. Henn). Wiley, Chichester.

Kennedy, J.L. *et al.* (1988). Evidence against linkage of schizophrenia to markers on chromosome 5 in a northern Swedish pedigree. *Nature*, **336**, 167–70.

Kety, S. (1959). Biochemical theories of schizophrenia I and II. *Science*, **129**, 1528, 1590.

Kety, S.S. and Schmidt, E.F. (1948). The nitrous oxide method for determination of cerebral bloodflow in man. *Journal of Clinical Investigation*, **27**, 476–83.

Kety, S.S., Rosenthal, D., Wender, P.I.L., Schulsinger, F., and Jacobsen, B. (1975).

Mental illness in the biologic and adoptive families of adopted individuals who become schizophrenic: a preliminary report based on psychiatric interviews. In *Genetic Research in psychiatry* (ed. R.R. Fieve, D. Rosenthal, and H. Brill). Johns Hopkins University Press, Baltimore.

Keuhl, F.A., Osmond, R.E., and Vendanheuvel, W.J.A. (1966). Occurrence of 3,4 dimethoxyphenylacetic acid in urines of normal and schizophrenic individuals. *Nature (London)*, **211**, 606.

Kim, J.S., Kornhuber, H.H., and Schmid-Burgk, W. (1980). Low cerebrospinal fluid glutamate in schizophrenic patients and a new hypothesis on schizophrenia. *Neuroscience Letters*, **20**, 379–82.

Kinnear (1727). Cited by Hunter, R. and Macalpine, I. (1968). *Three hundred years of psychiatry 1535–1860*. Oxford University Press.

Kleinberg, D.L., Wharton, R.N., and Frantz, A.G. (1971). Rapid release of prolactin in normal adults following chlorpromazine stimulation. *53rd Programme of Endocrine Society Meetings*, **126**, San Francisco.

Klippel, M. and Lhermitte, J. (1909). Un cas de démence précoce à type catatonique avec autopsie. *Revue Neurologique*, **17**, 157–8.

Kornhuber, J., Mack-Burkhardt, F., and Reiderer, P. (1989). [3H]MK-801 binding sites in postmortem brain regimes of schizophrenic patients. *Journal of Neural Transmitters*, **77**, 231–6.

Kottgen, C., Sonnichsen, I., Mollenhauer, K., and Jurth, R. (1984). Group therapy with the families of schizophrenic patients: results of the Hamburg Camberwell Family Interview Study, III. *International Journal of Family Psychiatry*, **5**, 84–94.

Kovelman, J.A. and Schiebel, A.B. (1984). A neurohistological correlate of schizophrenia. *Biological Psychiatry*, **19**, 1601–21.

Kraepelin, E. (1896). *Psychiatrie* (5th edn). Barth, Leipzig.

Kraepelin, E. (1899), *Psychiatrie. Ein Lehrbuch für Studierende und Ärtze* (6th edn). Barth, Leipzig.

Kraepelin, E. (1907). *Lehrbuch der Psychiatrie* (trans. A.R. Diefendorf). Macmillan, New York.

Kraepelin, E. (1919). *Dementia praecox* (trans. R.M. Barclay), (ed. G.M. Robertson). Facsimile edition published by Krieger, New York, 1971.

Krawiecka, M., Goldberg, D., and Vaughan, M. (1977). A standardised psychiatric assessment for rating chronic psychotic patients. *Acta Psychiatrica Scandinavica*, **55**, 299–308.

Kretchmer, E. (1936). *Physique and character*. Routledge, London.

Lader, M.H., Ron, M., and Petursson, H. (1984). Computerised axial brain tomography in long term benzodiazepine users. *Psychological Medicine*, **14**, 203–6.

Lancet (1978). The biochemistry of depression. *Lancet*, **i**, 422–3.

Lancet (1985). Psychiatry—a discipline that lost its way. *Lancet*, **i**, 731–2.

Lancet (1992). Atypical treatments for schizophrenia. *Lancet*, **339**, 276–77.

Langfeldt, G. (1960). Diagnosis and prognosis of schizophrenia. *Proceedings of the Royal Society of Medicine*, **53**, 1047–52.

Leary, J., Johnstone, E.C., and Owens, D.G.C. (1991). Social outcome, II. In disabilities and circumstances of schizophrenic patients—A follow up study. *British Journal of Psychiatry*, **159**, (Suppl. 13), 13–20.

Lee, T., Seeman, P., Tourtellotte, W.W., Farley, I.J., Horneykiewicz, O. (1978).

Binding of 3H-neuroleptics and 3H apomorphine in schizophrenic brains. *Nature (London)*, **274**, 897–900.

Leff, J.P. (1977). International variations in the diagnosis of psychiatric illness. *British Journal of Psychiatry*, **131**, 329–38.

Leff, J.P. and Vaughn, C. (1972). Psychiatric patients in contact and out of contact with services: a clinical and social assessment. In *Evaluating a community psychiatric service* (ed. J.K. Wing and A.M. Hailey). Oxford University Press.

Leff, J.P. and Vaughn, C.E. (1981). The role of maintenance therapy and relatives' expressed emotion in relapse in schizophrenia: a two year follow up. *British Journal of Psychiatry*, **139**, 102–4.

Leff, J.P. and Wing, J.K. (1981). Trial of maintenance therapy in schizophrenia. *British Medical Journal*, **3**, 599–604.

Leff, J.P. et al. (1987). The influence of relatives expressed emotion on the cause of schizophrenia in Chandighar. *British Journal of Psychiatry*, **151**, 166–73.

Leff, J.P. Berkowitz, R., Shavit, N, Strachan, A., Glass, I., and Vaughn, C. (1989). A trial of family therapy in a relatives group for schizophrenia. *British Journal of Psychiatry*, **154**, 58–66.

Lemke, R. (1935). Untersuchungen über die soziale Prognose der Schizophrenie unter besondener Berucksichtigung des encephalographischen Befundes. *Archiv für Psychiatrik Nervenkrank*, **104**, 89–136.

Lewine, R.J. (1981). Sex differences in schizophrenia: timing or subtypes. *Psychological Bulletin*, **90**, 432–44.

Lewis, N.D.C. (1923). The constitutional factors in dementia praecox with particular attention to the circulatory system and to some of the endocrine glands. *Nervous and Mental Diseases Monographs*, No. 35. Nervous and Mental Disease Publishing Co., New York.

Lewis, S.W. (1989). Congenital risk factors for schizophrenia. *Psychological Medicine*, **19**, 5–13.

Lidz, T., Fleck, S., and Cornelison, A.R. (1965). *Schizophrenia and the family*. International Universities Press, New York.

Lindenmayer, J.P. and Kay, S.R. (1992). Introduction. *New biological vistas on schizophrenia* (ed. J.P. Lindenmayer and S.R. Kay). Brunner Mazel, New York.

Luby, E.D., Gottlieb, J.S., Cohen, B.D., Rosenbaum, F. and Domino, E.F. (1962). Model psychosis and schizophrenia. *American Journal of Psychiatry*, **119**, 61–5.

Mackay, A.V.P. et al. (1982). Increased brain dopamine and dopamine receptors in schizophrenia. *Archives of General Psychiatry*, **39**, 991–7.

Mackenzie, I. (1912). The physical basis of mental disease. *Journal of Mental Science*, **58**, 465–77.

Macmillan, J.F., Crow, T.J., Johnson, A.L., and Johnstone, E.C. (1986a). The Northwick Park study of first episodes of schizophrenia. III: Short term outcome in trial entrants and trial eligible patients. *British Journal of Psychiatry*, **148**, 128–33.

Macmillan, J.F., Gold, A., Crow, T.J., Johnson, A.L., and Johnstone, E.C. (1986b). The Northwick Park first episodes study. IV: Expressed emotion and relapse. *British Journal of Psychiatry*, **148**, 133–44.

McClintock, F.H. and Avison, N.H. (1968). *Crime in England and Wales*. Heinemann, London.

McCreadie, R.G. (1982). The Nithsdale Schizophrenia Survey. I: Psychiatric and social handicaps. *British Journal of Psychiatry*, **140**, 582–6.

McCreadie, R.G. and Robinson, A.D.T. (1987). The Nithsdale Schizophrenia Survey. VI: Relatives expressed emotion prevalence patterns and clinical assessment. *British Journal of Psychiatry*, **150**, 640–4.

McGuffin, P. (1990). Models of heritability and genetic transmission. In *Search for the causes of schizophrenia*, Vol. II (ed. H. Hafner and W.F. Gattaz). Springer, Berlin.

McGuffin, P., Farmer, A.E., and Gottesman, I. (1987). Is there really a split in schizophrenia? The genetic evidence. *British Journal of Psychiatry*, **150**, 581–92.

McKenna, P.J., Tamlyn, D., Lund, C.E., Mortimer, A.M., Hammond, S., and Baddeley, A.D. (1990). Amnesic syndrome in schizophrenia. *Psychological Medicine*, **20**, 967–72.

McNeil (1987). Perinatal influences in the development of schizophrenia. In *Biological perspectives in schizophrenia* (ed. H. Helmchen and F.A. Henn). Wiley, Chichester.

McNeil, T.F. and Kaij, L. (1978). Obstetric factors in the development of schizophrenia: complications in the births of pre-schizophrenics and in reproduction by schizophrenic patients. In *The nature of schizophrenia* (ed. L.C. Wynne, R.L. Romwell, and E. Matthyss), pp. 401–29. Wiley, New York.

McNeill, T.H. and Sladek, J.R. (1978). Fluorescence – immunocytochemistry: simultaneous localization of catecholamines and gonadotrophen releasing hormone. *Science*, **200**, 72–4.

Marder, S.R. *et al.* (1984). Costs and benefits of two doses of fluphenazine. *Archives of General Psychiatry*, **41**, 1025.

Marks, V. and Rose, F.C. (1965). *Hypoglycaemia*. Blackwell, Oxford.

Marsden, C.D. (1976). Cerebral atrophy and cognitive impairment in chronic schizophrenia. *Lancet*, **ii**, 1079.

Martin, D. (1955). Institutionalisation. *Lancet*, **ii**, 1188–90.

Martin, J.B. (1973). Neural regulation of growth hormone secretion. *New England Journal of Medicine*, **288**, 1384–93.

Martin, J.B., Reichlin, S., and Brown, G.M. (1977). In *Clinical neuroendocrinology, contemporary neurology*. Davis, Philadelphia.

May, P.R.A. (1974). Treatment of schizophrenia iii a survey of the literature on prefrontal leucotomy. *Comprehensive Psychiatry*, **15**, 375–88.

May, P.R.A., Tuma, A.H., Dixon, W.J., Yale, C., Thiele, D.A., and Kraude, W.H. (1981). Schizophrenia: a follow up study of the results of five forms of treatment. *Archives of General Psychiatry*, **38**, 776–84.

Mednick, S.A., Schulsinger, F., Teasdale, T.W., Schulsinger, H., Venables, P.H., and Roxk, D.R. (1978). *Schizophrenia in high risk children: sex differences in predisposing mental illness*, pp. 169–97. Brunner Mazel, New York.

Mednick, S.A. and Silverton, L. (1988). High risk studies in the aetiology of schizophrenia. In *Handbook of schizophrenia* (ed. M.T. Tsuang and J.C. Simpson); Vol. 3. Elserier, Amsterdam.

Meltzer, H.Y. (1985). Dopamine and negative symptoms in schizophrenia: critique of the type I-II hypothesis. In *Controversies in schizophrenia: Changes and constances*. Guilford, New York.

Meltzer, H.Y. (1991). Atypical antipsychotic drugs. In *Current practices and future developments in the pharmacotherapy of mental disorders*, (ed. H. Meltzer and D. Nerozzi). Excerpta Medica, Amsterdam.

Meltzer, H.Y. and Fang, V.S. (1976). The effect of neuroleptics on serum prolactin in schizophrenic patients. *Archives of General Psychiatry*, **33**, 279–84.

Meltzer, H.Y., Goode, D.J., Schyre, P.M., Young, M., and Fang, V.S. (1979). Effects of clozapine on human serum prolactin levels. *Psychopharmacology*, **51**, 185–7.

Mendels, J. (1976). Lithium in the treatment of depression. *American Journal of Psychiatry*, **133**, 373–8.

Miller, R.J. and Hiley, C.R. (1974). Antimuscarinic properties of neuroleptics and drug-inducted Parkinsonism. *Nature (London)*, **248**, 596–7.

Miller, R.J., Horn, A.S., and Iversen, L.L. (1974). The action of neuroleptic drugs on dopamine stimulated adenosine cyclic 3′ 5′ monophosphate production in rat neostratum and limbic forebrain. *Molecular Pharmacology*, **10**, 759–66.

Moline, R.A. Singh, S., Morris, A., and Meltzer, H. (1985). Family expressed emotion and relapse in schizophrenia in 24 urban American patients. *American Journal of Psychiatry*, **151**, 314–20.

Montgomery, S.A. and Asberg, M. (1979). A new depression scale designed to be sensitive to change. *British Journal of Psychiatry*, **134**, 383–9.

Montgomery, S.A. and Green, M.C.D. (1988). The use of cholecystokinin in schizophrenia: a review. *Psychological Medicine*, **18**, 593–603.

Moore, M.T., Nathan, D., Elliott, A.R., and Laubach, C. (1933). Encephalographic studies in schizophrenia (dementia praecox): report of sixty cases. *American Journal of Psychiatry*, **12**, 801–10.

Morel, B.A. (1860) *Traite des maladies mentales*. Masson, Paris.

Morice, R. (1990). Cognitive inflexibility and prefrontal dysfunction in schizophrenia and mania. *British Journal of Psychiatry*, **157**, 50–4.

Mott, F.W. (1919). Normal and morbid conditions of the testes from birth to old age in 100 asylum and hospital cases. *British Medical Journal*, **ii**, 655–58.

Muller, E.E., Nistico, G., and Scapagini, E. (1977). In *Neurotransmitters and anterior pituitary function*. Academic Press, New York.

Murray, R.M. and Lewis, S.W. (1987). Is schizophrenia a neurodevelopmental disorder? *British Medical Journal*, **295**, 681–2.

Murray, R.M., and Lewis, S.W., and Reveley, M.A. (1985). Towards an aetiological classification of schizophrenia. *Lancet*, **i**, 1023–6.

Myerson, A. (1939). Theory and principles of the 'total push' method in the treatment of chronic schizophrenia. *American Journal of Psychiatry*, **95**, 1197–204.

Nagy, K. (1963). Pneumoencephalographische Befunde bei endogen Psychosen. *Nervenarzt*, **34**, 543–8.

Nasrallah, H.A., Jacoby, C.G., McCalley-Whitters, M., and Kuperman, S. (1982). Cerebral ventricular enlargement in subtypes of chronic schizophrenia. *Archives of General Psychiatry*, **39**, 773–7.

Nasrallah, H.A., Olson, S.C., McCalley-Whitters, M., Chapman, S., and Jacoby, C.G. (1986). Cerebral ventricular size in schizophrenia. A preliminary follow up study. *Archives of General Psychiatry*, **43**, 157–9.

Nelson, H.E. and O'Connell, A. (1978). Dementia: the estimation of premorbid intelligence levels using the New Adult Reading Test. *Cortex*, **14**, 234–44.

NIMH (National Institute of Mental Health), Psychopharmacology Service Center, Collaborative Study Group (1964). Phenothiazine treatment of acute schizophrenia. *Archives of General Psychiatry*, **10**, 246–61.

NSF (National Schizophrenia Fellowship) (1979). *Home sweet nothing. The plight of sufferers from chronic schizophrenia.* NSF, London.

Nelson, H.E., Pantelis, C., Carruthers, K., Speller, J., Baxendale, S., and Barnes, T.R.E. (1990). Cognitive functioning and symptomatology in chronic schizophrenia. *Psychological Medicine*, **20**, 357–65.

NWTRHA (North West Thames Regional Health Authority) (1985). *Draft regional strategy.* NWTRHA, London.

Nutt, D. (1990). Specific anatomy: non specific drugs: the present state of schizophrenia. *Journal of Psychopharmacology*, **4**, 171–5.

O'Callaghan, E., Sham, P., Takei, N., Glover, G., and Murray, R.M. (1991). Schizophrenia after prenatal exposure to 1957 A2 influenza epidemic. *Lancet*, **337**, 1248–50.

Owen, M.J. and Lewis, S.W. (1986). Lateral ventricular size in schizophrenia. *Lancet*, **ii**, 223–4.

Owen, F., Cross, A.J., Crow, T.J., Longden, A., Poulter, M., and Riley, G.J. (1978). Increased dopamine receptor sensitivity in schizophrenia. *Lancet*, **ii**, 223–6.

Owen, F., Cross, A.J., Crow, T.J., Lofthouse, R., and Poulter, M. (1981). Neurotransmitter receptors in the brain in schizophrenia. *Acta Psychiatrica Scandinavica*, **62** (suppl 291), 20–26..

Owens, D.G.C. (1992). Imaging aspects of the biology of schizophrenia. In *Current Opinion in Psychiatry*, **5**, 6–14.

Owens, D.G.C. and Johnstone, E.C. (1980). The disabilities of chronic schizophrenia—their nature and factors contributing to their development. *British Journal of Psychiatry*, **136**, 384–95.

Owens, D.G.C., Johnstone, E.C., and Frith, C.D. (1982). Spontaneous involuntary disorders of movement: their prevalance, severity and distribution in chronic schizophrenics with and without treatment with neuroleptics. *Archives of General Psychiatry*, **39**, 452–61.

Owens, D.G.C., Johnstone, E.C., Crow, T.J., Frith, C.D., Jagoe, J.R., and Kreel, L.L. (1985). Lateral ventricular size in schizophrenia. Relationships to the disease process and its clinical manifestations. *Psychological Medicine*, **15**, 27–41.

Parker, G., Johnston, P., and Hayward, L. (1988). Parental 'expressed emotion' as a predictor of schizophrenic relapse. *Archives of General Psychiatry*, **45**, 806–13.

Perry, T.L. (1982). Normal cerebrospinal fluid and brain glutamate levels in schizophrenia do not support the hypothesis of glutamatergic neuronal dysfunction. *Neuroscience Letters*, **28**, 81–5.

Persons, J.B., (1986). The advantages of studying psychological phenomena rather than psychiatric diagnoses. *American Journal of Psychology*, **41**, 1252–60.

Pinel, P. (1809). *Traité medico-philosophique sur l'aliénation mental* (2nd edn). Brosson, Paris.

Pogue-Geile, M.F. and Zubin, J. (1988). Negative symptomatology and schizophrenia. A conceptual and empirical review. *International Journal of Mental Health*, **16**, 3–45.

Pope, H.G. and Lipinski, J.F. (1978). Diagnosis of schizophrenia and manic depressive illness: a reassessment of the specificity of 'schizophrenic' symptoms in the light of current research. *Archives of General Psychiatry*, **35**, 811–28.

Posner, M.I., Petersen, S.E., Fox, P.T., and Raichle, M.E. (1988). Localisation of cognitive operations in the human brain. *Science*, **240**, 1627–31.

Post, R.M. (1982). Carbamazepine's acute and prophylactic effects in manic and depressive illness. An update. *International Drug Therapy Newsletter*, **17**, 5–9.

Post, R.M., Fink, E., Carpenter, W.T., and Goodwin, F.K. (1975). Cerebrospinal fluid amine metabolism in acute schizophrenia. *Archives of General Psychiatry*, **32**, 1013–69.

Prien, R.J. (1979). Lithium in the treatment of schizo affective disorders. *Archives of General Psychiatry*, **36**, 852–3.

Prien, R.F., Caffey, E.M., and Klett, C.J. (1972a). Comparison of lithium carbonate and chlorpromazine in the treatment of mania. *Archives of General Psychiatry*, **26**, 146–53.

Prien, R.F., Caffey, E.M., and Klett, C.J. (1972b). A comparison of lithium carbonate and chlorpromazine in the treatment of excited schizo affectives: report of the Veterans Administration and National Institute of Mental Health Collaborative Study Group. *Archives of General Psychiatry*, **27**, 182–9.

Procci, W.R. (1976). Schizo affective psychosis: fact or fiction. *Archives of General Psychiatry*, **33**, 1167–78.

Randrup, A. and Munkvad, I. (1965). Special antagonism of amphetamine-induced abnormal behaviour. Inhibition of stereotyped activity with increase of some normal activities. *Psychopharmacologia*, **7**, 416–22.

Rees, W.L. (1950). Body size, personality and neurosis. *Journal of Mental Science*, **96**, 168–80.

Renfrew, S. (1967). *An introduction to diagnostic neurology—a course of instruction for students*, Vols I and II. Livingstone, Edinburgh.

Roberts, G.W. and Crow, T.J. (1987). The neuropathology of schizophrenia: a progress report. *British Medical Bulletin*, **43**, 599–615.

Roberts, G.W., Bruton, C.J., and Crow, T.J. (1988). Gliosis in schizophrenia. *Biological Psychiatry*, **24**, 729–30.

Ron, M.A., Acker, W., Shaw, G.K., and Lishman, W.A. (1982) Computerised tomography of the brain in chronic alcoholism—a survey and follow up study. *Brain*, **105**, 497–14.

Rosanoff, A.J. (1914). Dissimilar heredity in mental disease. *American Journal of Insanity*, **LXX**, 1.

Rosenthal, D., Wender, P.H., Kety, S.S., Welner, J., and Schulsinger, F. (1971). The adopted away offspring of schizophrenics. *American Journal of Psychiatry*, **128**, 397–411.

St. Clair, D. *et al.* (1989). No linkage of chromosome 5q11–q13 markers to schizophrenia in Scottish families. *Nature*, **339**, 305–9.

Scharfstein, S.S. (1978). Will community mental health survive in the 1980s? *American Journal of Psychiatry*, **135**, 1363–1365.

Schou, M. (1963). Normothymics, 'mood normalisers'. Are lithium and imipramine drugs specific for affective disorders? *British Journal of Psychiatry*, **109**, 803–9.

Schneider, K. (1957a). *Klinische Psychopathologie* (5th edn), (trans. M.W. Hamilton). Grune and Stratton, New York.

Schneider, K. (1957*b*). Primäre und secundäre Symptome bei der Schizophrenie. *Fortschritte in Neurologischen und Psychiatrischan Grenzgebieten*, **25**, 487–90.

Seeman, P. (1980). Brain dopamine receptors. *Pharmacological Reviews*, **32**, 229–313.

Seeman, P., Lee, T., Chau-Wong, M., and Wong, K. (1976). Antipsychotic drug doses and neuroleptic dopamine receptors. *Nature (London)*, **261**, 717–19.

Shallice, T., Burgess, P.W., and Frith, C.D. (1991). Can the neuropsychological case-study approach be applied to schizophrenia? *Psychological Medicine*, **21**, 661–73.

Shattock, F.M. (1950). The somatic manifestations of schizophrenia: a clinical study of their significance. *Journal of Mental Science*, **96**, 32–142.

Sherrington, R. *et al.* (1988). Localisation of a susceptibility locus for schizophrenia on chromosome 5. *Nature*, **336**, 164–7.

Singh, M.M. and Kay, S.R. (1975). Therapeutic reversal with benztropine in schizophrenics. *Journal of Nervous and Mental Disease*, **160**, 258–66.

Small, J.G., Kellams, J.J., Milstein, V., and Moore, J. (1975). A placebo controlled study of lithium combined with neuroleptics in chronic schizophrenic patients. *American Journal of Psychiatry*, **132**, 1315–17.

Smith, G.N. and Iacono, W.G. (1986). Lateral ventricular size in schizophrenia and choice of control group. *Lancet*, **i**, 1450.

Snyder, S.H., Greenberg, D., and Yamamura, H.I. (1974). Antischizophrenic drugs and brain cholinergic receptors. *Archives of General Psychiatry*, **31**, 58–61.

Sokoloff, P., Giros, B., Martres, M.P., Bouthenet, M.L., and Schwartz, J.C. (1990). Molecular cloning and characterization of a novel dopamine receptor (D3) as a target for neuroleptics. *Nature*, **347**, 146–51.

Southard, E.E. (1915). On the topographical distribution of cortex lesions and anomalies in dementia praecox with some account of their functional significance, II. *American Journal of Insanity*, **71**, 603–71.

Spitzer, R.L., Endicott, J., and Robins, E. (1975). Clinical criteria for psychiatric diagnosis and DSM III. *American Journal of Psychiatry*, **132**, 1187–92.

Spitzer, R.L., Endicott, J., and Robins, E. (1977). *Research diagnostic criteria for a selected group of functional disorders* (3rd edn). Biometrics Research Division, New York State Psychiatric Institute.

Stevens, J.R. (1982). Neuropathology of schizophrenia. *Archives of General Psychiatry*, **39**, 1131–9.

Stevens, J., Casanova, M., and Bigelow, L. (1988). Gliosis in schizophrenia. *Biological Psychiatry*, **24**, 727–9.

Stevens, M., Crow, T.J., Bowman, M.J., and Coles, E.C. (1978). Age disorientation in schizophrenia: a constant prevalence of 25 per cent in a chronic mental hospital population? *British Journal of Psychiatry*, **112**, 135–44.

Stokes, P.E., Stoll, P.M., Shamoian, C.A., and Patton, M.J. (1971). Efficacy of lithium as acute treatment of manic depressive illnesses. *Lancet*, **i**, 1319–25.

Storey, P.B. (1966). Lumbar air encephalography in chronic schizophrenia: a controlled experiment. *British Journal of Psychiatry*, **112**, 135–44.

Sturt, J. and Waters, H. (1985). Role of the psychiatrist in community based mental health care. *Lancet*, **i**, 507–9.

Sunahara, R.K. *et al.* (1991). Cloning of the gene for a human dopamine D5 receptor with high affinity for dopamine than D1. *Nature*, **350**, 614–19.

Swazey, J.P. (1974). *Chlorpromazine in psychiatry: a study of therapeutic innovation*. MIT Press, Cambridge, Mass.

Tamlyn, D., McKenna, P.J., Mortimer, A.M., Lund, C.E., Hammond, S., and Baddeley, A.D. (1992). Memory impairment in schizophrenia: its extent, affiliations and neuropsychological character. *Psychological Medicine*, **22**, 101–15.

Tamminga, C.A., Littman, R.L., and Alphs, L.D. (1986). Cholecystokinin. A neuropeptide in the treatment of schizophrenia. *Psychopharmacology Bulletin*, **22**, 129–31.

Tarrier, N. *et al.* (1989). Community management of schizophrenia. A two year follow up of behavioural intervention with families. *British Journal of Psychiatry*, **154**, 625–8.

Taylor, G.R., Crow, T.J., Ferrier, I.N., Johnstone, E.C., Parry, R.P., and Tyrrell, D.A.J. (1982). Virus-like agent in CSF in schizophrenia and some neurological disorders. *Lancet*, **ii**, 1166–7.

Taylor, the Lord (1962). The public, parliament and mental health. *In Aspects of psychiatric Research* (ed. D. Richter, J.M. Tanner, Lord Taylor and P.L. Zangmill). Oxford University Press, London.

Tidmarsh, D. (1990). Schizophrenia. In *Principles and practice of forensic medicine*, (ed. R Bluglass and P. Bowden), pp. 321–43. Churchill-Livingstone, London.

Tooth, G.C. and Brooke, E.M. (1961). Trends in the mental hospital population and their effect on future planning. *Lancet*, **i**, 710–13.

Toru, M., Watanabe, S., and Shibuy, A.H. (1988). Neurotransmitters, receptors and neuropeptides in post-mortem brains of chronic schizophrenic patients. *Acta Psychiatrica Scandinavica*, **78**, 121–37.

Turner, J. (1912). The classification of insanity. *Journal of Mental Science*, **58**, 1–25.

Van Tol, H.H.M. *et al.* (1991). Cloning of the gene for a human dopamine D4 receptor with high affinity for the antipsychotic clozapine. *Nature*, **350**, 610–14.

Vaughn, C.E. and Leff, J.P. (1976). The influence of family and social factors on the course of psychiatric illness: a comparison of schizophrenic and depressed neurotic patients. *British Journal of Psychiatry*, **129**, 125–37.

Vaughn, C.E., Snyder, K.S., Jones, S., Freeman, W.B., and Falloon, I.R.H. (1984). Family factors in schizophrenic relapse: a California replication of the British research in expressed emotion. *Archives of General Psychiatry*, **41**, 1169–77.

Vogt, C. and Vogt, O. (1948). Über anatomische Substrate. Bemerkungen zu pathoanatomischen Befunden bei Schizophrenie. *Ärztliche Forschungen*, **3**, 1–7.

Wagner, H.N. *et al.* (1983). Imaging dopamine receptors in the human brain by position tomography, *Science*, **221**, 1264–6.

Wallace, M. (1983). Bedsit despair of the mental hospital outcasts. *Sunday Times*, 20 November.

Watt, D.C., Katz, K., and Shepherd, M. (1983). The natural history of schizophrenia; a 5 year prospective 5-year follow up of a representative sample of schizophrenics by means of a standardized clinical and social assessment. *Psychological Medicine*, **13**, 663–70.

Weinberger, D.R., Wagner, R.L., and Wyatt, R.J. (1983). Neuropathological studies of schizophrenia: a selective review. *Schizophrenia Bulletin*, **9**, 193–212.

Weinberger, D.R., Torrey, E.F., Neophytides, N., and Wyatt, R.J. (1979). Lateral ccrebral ventricular enlargement in chronic schizophrenia. *Archives of General Psychiatry*, **36**, 735–9.

Weller, M.P.I. (1985). Friern Hospital: Where have all the patients gone? *Lancet*, **i**, 569–71.

Welner, A., Croughan, J.L., and Robins, E. (1974). A group of schizoaffective related psychoses—critique, second follow up and family studies. *Archives of General Psychiatry*, **31**, 628–31.

Wernicke, C. (1900). *Grundriss der Psychiatrie*. Johannes Barth, Leipzig.

Willis, T. (1683). *Two discourses concerning the soul of brutes*. Dring, London.

Wing, J.K. (1961). A simple and reliable subclassification of chronic schizophrenia. *Journal of Mental Science*, **107**, 862–75.

Wing, J.K. (1989). The concept of negative symptoms. *British Journal of Psychiatry*, **155** (Suppl. 7), 10–14.

Wing, J.K. and Brown, G.W. (1961). Social treatment of chronic schizophrenia: a comparative survey of three mental hospitals. *Journal of Mental Science*, **107**, 847–61.

Wing, J.K. and Brown, G.W. (1970). *Institutionalism and schizophrenia*. Cambridge University Press.

Wing, J.K., Cooper, J.E., and Sartorius, N. (1974). *The description and classification of psychiatric symptoms. An instruction manual for the PSE and Catego systems*. Cambridge University Press.

Winslow, W.W. (1979). The changing role of the psychiatrist in community mental health centers. *American Journal of Psychiatry*, **136**, 24–7.

Withers, E. and Hinton, J. (1971). Three forms of the clinical tests of the sensorium and their reliability. *British Journal of Psychiatry*, **119**, 1–8.

Wong, D.F. *et al.* (1986). Position emission tomography reveals elevated D2 dopamine receptors in drug naive schizophrenics. *Science*, **234**, 1558–63.

Young, I.J. and Crampton, A.R. (1974). Cerebrospinal fluid uric acid levels in cerebral atrophy occurring in psychiatric and neurologic patients. *Biological Psychiatry*, **8**, 281–92.

Young, I.R., Hall, A.S., Pallis, C.A., Bydder, G.M., Legg, N.J., and Steiner, R.E. (1981). Nuclear magnetic resonance of the brain in multiple sclerosis. *Lancet*, **2**, 1063–6.

Zitrin, A. *et al.* (1976). Crime and violence among mental patients. *American Journal of Psychiatry*, **133**, 142–9.

Zukin, S.R. and Javitt, D.C. (1992). The PCP/NMDA theory of schizophrenia. In *New biological vistas on schizophrenia* (ed. J.P. Lindenmayer and S.R. Kay). Brunner Mazel, New York.

Zukin, S.R. and Zukin R.S. (1979). Specific [3H] phencyclidine binding in rat central nervous system. *Proceedings of the National Academy of Sciences (USA)*, **76**, 5372–6.

Index